"*Fusion Strategy* will be the definitive way for industrial companies to win against new competitors. The authors have masterfully captured the crux of what should be done over the next decade."

— **INDRA K. NOOYI,** former Chairman and CEO, PepsiCo; Member of the Board, Amazon

"Fusion Strategy is a masterpiece on the topic of harnessing the power of data and AI to survive and to thrive. We are recommending that every one of our clients, from the boardroom to the C-suite to managers across all functions, read this book."

— **LINDA YATES,** founder and CEO, Mach49

"The authors have studied how digital companies have won in the asset-light segments of the economy, and they share practical wisdom on how to navigate and win in this environment. *Fusion Strategy* will become part of the vocabulary of how we think about winning."

— **MARC N. CASPER,** Chairman, President, and CEO, Thermo Fisher Scientific

"*Fusion Strategy* moves beyond the buzzword hype around data and AI and brings much-needed clarity and strategic direction to the backbone of our economy—the industrial sector."

— **MARC BITZER,** CEO, Whirlpool Corporation

"I would strongly recommend that executives in industrial businesses read this book and learn how to integrate hardware and software to create customer value."

— **VIMAL KAPUR,** CEO, Honeywell

"*Fusion Strategy* gives us a compelling vision for the next wave of digitization, one that combines new technologies—like AI and machine learning—with the legacy economy. Fusion strategies will be the new competitive battlefield. This is a great book."

— **JEFF IMMELT,** former Chairman and CEO, General Electric; Venture Partner, New Enterprise Associates

"*Fusion Strategy* helps leaders understand how to create competitive advantage through collaborative intelligence—embracing the power of data, AI, and other digital technologies. This is going to be central to unlocking value creation and securing the future success of every company."

—**SHAILESH JEJURIKAR,** Chief Operating Officer, Procter & Gamble

"With its blend of practical advice, compelling case studies, and clear writing, *Fusion Strategy* is a must-read for leaders in industrial companies seeking to navigate disruptive change. Highly recommended."

—**SCOTT D. ANTHONY,** Senior Partner, Innosight; author, *Dual Transformation* and *Eat, Sleep, Innovate*

"*Fusion Strategy* is a guide to unlocking significant value by codifying competitive advantages in the form of datagraphs. This book is a road map to staying relevant."

—**QUE DALLARA,** former President and CEO, Honeywell Connected Enterprise; Executive Vice President and President, Diabetes Operating Unit, Medtronic

"This is a book for business leaders to understand the power of data and AI without excessive jargon and technical language. A must-read to learn the opportunities for unlocking trapped business value by fusing the real and the digital worlds."

—**PETER KOERTE,** Chief Technology Officer and Chief Strategy Officer, Siemens AG, Germany

"This book provides an excellent and practical framework for global companies to create their own fusion strategy. Govindarajan and Venkatraman have pointed corporations toward a North Star during some of the most challenging times."

—**KINYA SETO,** President and CEO, LIXIL, Japan

"Reading *Fusion Strategy* has been a truly mind-expanding experience for me. Based on their extensive empirical research and deep reflection, Govindarajan and Venkatraman have shown us the spectacular possibilities of the fusion of industrial production with breakthrough digital technologies, driven by intelligent machines that are not only smart but brilliant."

—**MUKESH D. AMBANI,** Chairman and Managing Director, Reliance Industries Limited, India

"*Fusion Strategy* is an important book for our leaders as it makes the case that real-time insights have now surpassed assets as the most valuable competitive advantage that every company must seek."

—**N. CHANDRASEKARAN,** Chairman, Tata Sons; former CEO, Tata Consultancy Services, India

"Fusion future is already here. This timely book lays out the compelling logic of how industrial giants can transform from analog to digital insight companies. I highly recommend this book to leaders in every industrial company."

—**ANAND MAHINDRA,** Chairman, Mahindra Group, India

"This book advances compelling, fresh thinking about how industrial incumbents must compete to win. Hence the relevance of *Fusion Strategy* for India—not just for Indian corporations but also for policy-makers—to make India a global hub for smart industrial strategy."

—**SUDARSHAN VENU,** Managing Director, TVS Motor Company, India

"The timing of *Fusion Strategy* couldn't be more opportune. It serves as a beacon, illustrating and guiding leaders in industrials on the path to harnessing AI technology in the creation of smart products through smart processes."

—**JOSH FOULGER,** Managing Director, Bharat FIH, India

"The concept of rich industrial datagraphs that scale outside the company is a very powerful thought in developing customer-centric value creation strategies, going well beyond using digital to achieve cost leadership and product enhancement. I'm sure this book will stimulate thinking and action in many industrial companies to move from products to fusion solutions. I thoroughly enjoyed reading *Fusion Strategy*, and it will form an important reference point as I think about strategy and value creation going forward."

—**T. V. NARENDRAN,** CEO and Managing Director, Tata Steel, India

"Fusion Strategy is a timely reminder that how we do business in the B2B space has been transformed forever with the arrival of digital technologies and AI. Embracing this reality and developing a fusion strategy mindset will help industrial companies differentiate and unlock new value. Understanding the role of datagraphs and AI proficiency, and of the fusion between the physical and digital ecosystems, the next battlegrounds, and the importance of networks in delivering longer-term value will all play an important role. This thought-provoking (and action-inspiring) book has provided me with excellent strategic insight."

—**EDMOND SCANLON,** CEO, Kerry Group, Ireland

FUSION
STRATEGY

HOW
REAL-TIME
DATA AND **AI**
WILL POWER THE
INDUSTRIAL
FUTURE

VIJAY GOVINDARAJAN
VENKAT VENKATRAMAN

HARVARD BUSINESS REVIEW PRESS • BOSTON, MASSACHUSETTS

Copyright 2024 Vijay Govindarajan and Venkat Venkatraman

All rights reserved

Printed in the United States of America

10 9 8 7 6 5 4 3 2 1

No part of this publication may be reproduced, stored in or introduced into a retrieval system, or transmitted, in any form, or by any means (electronic, mechanical, photocopying, recording, or otherwise), without the prior permission of the publisher. Requests for permission should be directed to permissions@harvardbusiness.org, or mailed to Permissions, Harvard Business School Publishing, 60 Harvard Way, Boston, Massachusetts 02163.

The web addresses referenced in this book were live and correct at the time of the book's publication but may be subject to change.

Cataloging-in-Publication data is forthcoming.

ISBN: 978-1-64782-625-3
eISBN: 978-1-64782-626-0

The paper used in this publication meets the requirements of the American National Standard for Permanence of Paper for Publications and Documents in Libraries and Archives Z39.48-1992.

*To my granddaughters—Meera Govinda Stepinski (four years old),
Leila Raja Mirandi (nine months old), and Anya Govinda
Stepinski (six months old)—digital natives who will most
appreciate this book (if only they could read it!).*

—VG

*To the women in my life—my mother; my wife, Meera;
and my daughters, Tara and Uma—who all infuse digital
into their lives in unique ways.*

—Venkat

CONTENTS

PART ONE

WHEN STEEL MEETS SILICON

CHAPTER 1

The Industrial Past
Was Prologue

ONE HUNDRED TRILLION. WITH A T. THAT'S THE WORLD'S gross domestic product. Almost 75 percent of it was created by traditional manufacturing, mining, transportation, logistics, construction, and health care industries. Those sectors haven't been significantly changed by digital technologies yet. But they will be affected. Soon.

Ask the market leaders in physical asset-light sectors—such as advertising, photography, music, media, and entertainment—about digital technologies' impact, and the unanimous reply will be that the foundations of their industries have been transformed. Those market leaders that misread the signals about the importance of digital technologies on their business strategies, meanwhile, ended up losing their positions to born-digital companies. Relative upstarts like Netflix and Spotify have become the rule makers, harnessing the power of user data and AI to develop new sources of competitive advantage.

For a while, there was a feeling that digital technologies' impact would be limited to asset-light, high-information sectors. The cycles of innovation, disruption, and transformation over the last two decades happened in business-to-consumer (B2C) industries, thanks mainly to mobile technologies.

Business is now at the next inflection point, with advances in hardware, software, applications, cloud, data, algorithms, generative artificial intelligence (Gen AI), mixed reality, and other technologies on the horizon. These technologies—individually and in combination—are poised to reshape the global economy. And while these technologies do pose a threat to profitability, they will also be the biggest driver of how value creation and value capture evolve in every industry worldwide. That's why $75 trillion, 75 percent of the world's gross domestic product and the addressable market for digitalizing the industrial world, matters.

History may remember our present moment as the point when the industrial world's digitalization began in earnest after several false starts. To paraphrase Shakespeare, this pivotal point will show that the past is prologue, and the future is unfolding fast.

The world has codified, or digitized, only a fraction of its data and content so far. (See figure 1-1.) The fusion frontier is a future state in which industrial products are infused with sensors, software, and real-time telematic functionalities through the seamless convergence of physical and digital domains. This allows for enhancing the productivity of industrial assets and delivering personalized approaches to solving business problems with algorithms that make use of data observed across different settings. In this frontier, industrial companies excel not by simply designing and delivering brilliant machines but by ensuring that their machines satisfy the specific needs of individual customers. In this fusion frontier, much more could be codified in the future, such as health and wellness records, data on the operations of energy grids, maps of transportation in cities, occupancy of commercial and residential buildings, dashboards on farming and agriculture, distribution of food and supplies, and so on.

All of that will be enabled by computing capability in the form of quantum computing and more-powerful devices and systems in in-

FIGURE 1-1

The fusion frontier propelled by increased compute capability and opportunity to codify content

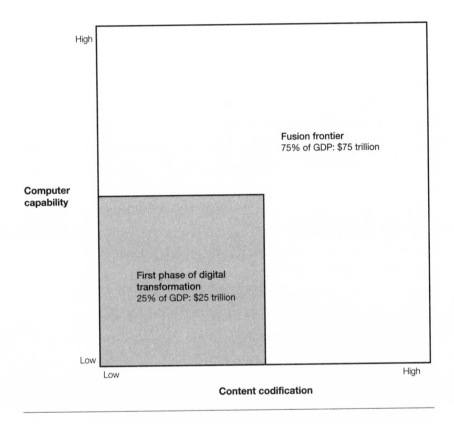

dustrial locations connected to the cloud. The question is, How do industrials capture this new value?

Over the past four years, we've studied digital giants, startups, and industrial manufacturers in asset-light and asset-heavy industries. We've conducted extensive interviews with a wide range of C-suite executives in a number of companies—such as Ford, Dover, Danaher, Mercedes-Benz, John Deere, DJI, GE, GM, Honeywell, Mahindra & Mahindra, Rolls-Royce, Samsung, Siemens, LIXIL, TVS Motor, and Whirlpool—and we've worked with some of them. Based on our case research and a longitudinal analysis of how digital technologies are evolving in business, we've developed a way of thinking about them that will help industrial companies compete and win tomorrow.

We call it *fusion*.

Going forward, industrials will need to combine what they do best (create physical products) with what digitals do best (use AI to parse enormous, interconnected, product-in-use datasets) to make strategic connections that would otherwise be impossible.

Consider John Deere, which has built a competitive advantage by producing faster, stronger, and bigger machines. Today Deere is preparing for the digital future. The company's See & Spray device revolutionizes herbicide use by shifting from blanket to targeted spot spraying. The self-propelled device uses a large carbon-fiber boom lined with thirty-six cameras that scan at incredible speeds. Powered by ten vision processing units that handle four gigabytes of data per second, this system utilizes deep learning to distinguish crops from weeds. Once a weed is identified, a command to kill it is sent to a nozzle even as the sprayer moves through the field at up to fifteen miles per hour. While initial versions detected only green weeds in bare fields, the newer version detects weeds of any color next to crops. The result: customer profits are boosted while herbicide use is reduced by 60 percent.

The innovation here is not in industrial machinery. It's in merging the digital and industrial domains with data and AI—a significant shift for a company like Deere that has designed only big industrial machines in the past.

This is just the beginning. The laws of competitive advantage are changing, rewarding those who have the most-robust real-time insights rather than the most-valuable physical assets. By taking a fusion approach, companies can improve their offerings' value to customers and develop innovative new products, novel services, and whole new ways of solving problems.

Ultimately, the combination of AI and real-time data will lead to a new generation of business models that will turbocharge products, strategies, and customer relationships. If companies adopt fusion strategies, they'll be able to capture incredible new value. If they don't, they'll be left behind.

Datagraphs Underpin Fusion

The goal of this book is to explain how business is rapidly changing and, ultimately, to show you how to use real-time data and AI to create your own fusion strategies. But how?

It all starts with data, the crux of fusion. Not just any data, but real-time data on products in use. By systematically accumulating such data, companies can develop *datagraphs*, which capture the relationships, links, and interrelationships between a company and its customers through product-in-use data and are the fundamental building blocks of the fusion strategies we explore in this book. We'll go into detail in the next two chapters, but here's a preview. The concept of the datagraph is inspired by social networks and graph theory, and powered by AI and machine learning (ML). Datagraphs are derived from *data network effects*, which are triggered when a company's product gets smarter as it gathers more data from users of the product.

For example, Google's search engine gets more intelligent as more individuals query with different search terms. Facebook's ability to deliver targeted content and ads is driven by the data network effects contributed by nearly three billion individuals.

A virtuous cycle kicks in. If consumers find these enhancements relevant and valuable, they are more likely to keep using the product, and in doing so, perpetuate the cycle. This creates a data bond between products and customers that deepens over time. Interconnections occur at the point of use; recommendations are customized to the context of those interactions; and value is created when the recommendations optimize consumer outcomes.

Datagraphs aren't static schematics, but rather dynamic representations whose algorithmic underpinnings help to absorb more data, analyze more kinds of data, and advise on specific actions. The sooner a company starts gathering product-in-use data to feed its business algorithms, the earlier its systems will generate data-driven decisions, the quicker it can act on them—and the more likely it is to stay ahead of rivals.

Datagraph-based advantage redefines scale and scope—two key concepts in strategy.[1] In the industrial era, companies expanded their scale of operations by increasing sales, which resulted in higher market shares. The process was linear and gradual, based on the company's ability to access physical, human, and financial capital. In contrast, datagraph-driven scale stems from orchestrating an ecosystem whose members play complementary roles. For instance, GM's scale is the number of automobiles it can manufacture, while Uber's scale is the number of rides it can arrange within its fast-evolving ecosystem.

We've all seen the signs that read, "Over *x* Billion Served" in front of every McDonald's outlet. Yet tracking the number of burgers sold each day, month, or year is a relic of the past. Datagraph leaders aren't concerned with absolute numbers alone; they want the details. They ask about who eats those burgers: Do we have data on where each consumer buys a burger? At what time? What do they do before or after that? What do they drink with it? What do we know about their age, sex, income, location, preferences, and lifestyles, so we can satisfy more of their needs? How can we make them spend more dollars on our platform, feel satisfied that they received value, and ensure they return to us?

Above all, there's a difference between digitals and industrials regarding the data they study.[2] Uber analyzes data on more than twenty-five billion rides, which the taxi companies don't. Netflix tracks people's viewing preferences by the second, which the cable and television companies don't. And Airbnb tracks where, when, and how long travelers stay and what they do and prefer, which the hotel chains don't.

Scope isn't about adjacencies anymore. An industrial expands the range of its activities by leveraging its capabilities to enter adjacent sectors; it builds physical infrastructure, acquires talent, and incurs additional capital. However, Apple, Amazon, and Google collect, organize, and analyze data to expand the scope of their businesses into many unrelated sectors. Datagraphs put AI-driven problem-solving capabilities in reach of nearly any business. The digitals have displayed this capability in physical asset-light settings, and they could influence physical asset-heavy settings.

That's a warning sign for the industrials. Datagraph-driven insights allow the digitals to expand and grow, so it's time for the industrials to start thinking about increasing their operations' scale and scope exponentially.

Algorithms Animate Fusion

Datagraphs are one part of the story. To be valuable, algorithms must analyze them to develop actionable recommendations.

To begin with, executives can conduct descriptive analyses to understand *what* happened with a product or service. Then, they can carry out diagnostic analyses by drilling down to the root cause of the outcomes, essentially identifying the *why* behind the *what*. These are historical analyses akin to looking at a rearview mirror.

Next are predictive analyses, based on datagraphs, to forecast future events with different levels of probability, informed by data from the entire customer base. And finally, prescriptive analyses offer recommended actions. When these four analyses—descriptive, diagnostic, predictive, and prescriptive—are carried out on datagraphs that build on data network effects, they offer deep and powerful insights.

Real-time data that feeds datagraphs and algorithms will help industrial companies win in the fusion future. There's no fusion strategy without datagraphs; there's no business value in datagraphs without authoritative algorithms. Fusion strategy is built on both datagraphs *and* AI.

Fusion Is the Future

Yes, fusion means using datagraphs, AI, and algorithms. But it also means so much more.

In a general sense, fusion is the process or the result of joining two or more things to form a single entity. Scientifically inclined readers might define fusion as causing a material or object to melt with intense heat to join another. Musicians use the word to describe a combination of styles, such as jazz and rock, or Western and Indian classical. Chefs use the term to describe cooking that incorporates elements of different cuisines, such as French and Japanese, or Italian and Indian.

In the context of digitalizing industrial sectors, fusion consists of five strands.

1. *The interlocking of the physical and digital business domains, seamlessly blending functions that were historically separated.* The modern automobile is a computer on wheels that's connected to the cloud. Tractors are becoming industrial machines driven by intelligent agronomists. The latest buildings are architectural marvels with autonomous control systems.

2. *The intertwining of humans and machines to work together in creating the next frontier of expertise and insights.* Companies that leverage the collective intelligence of smart humans and powerful machines will win against those that haven't taken advantage of the collaboration.

3. *The infusion of digital thinking into the analog disciplines of sciences, arts, and engineering.* Until recently, computing and algorithms were regarded as distinct from medicine, law, psychology, economics, and finance. Now every discipline is being informed and impacted by digital. Agriculture's future is sustainable farming enabled by sensors and software. Medicine's frontier is personalized health with biomarkers and customized

cures. Education is being transformed with personalized tutoring supported by AI.

4. *The interlinking of physical and virtual worlds through the cloud, gaining real-time insights with digital twins, mixed reality, and metaverses.* Combining physical and digital worlds will add 1 percent or more annually to the global gross domestic product over the next decade.[3] Beyond the gains to efficiency and timeliness, this advance also makes for a healthier planet, primarily by reducing wasteful use of scarce resources.

5. *The interconnections among companies, with a corporation becoming a portfolio of capabilities through cross-industry ecosystems.* Every company already relies on a network of partners to be successful. Digital technologies—especially data interconnections—will make products perform better, ensure that business processes are more streamlined, and help deliver superior customer service.

These *fusion forces*, as we call them, will shape and reshape the future of the industrial world. They were previously unavailable at affordable price-performance levels. But with the rise of powerful sensors, greater computing power, and artificial intelligence, things are changing fast.

Just look at the automobile industry.

Automobiles Lead the Way

As author William Gibson said: "The future is already here—it's just not very evenly distributed."

In the automobile industry, the analog product has progressively become digital; mobility as a service becomes economically feasible with data network effects instead of asset ownership. For example, without real-time data on the location and availability of different transportation options, we could not have created ride-sharing networks at affordable price points. We use this sector as an example throughout the book because it's an industry that most readers can relate to and that offers significant lessons and implications for other industrial sectors.

By January 2024, it was common to see autonomous cars drive by in San Francisco—some with test drivers at the wheel and others without—picking up riders and taking them to their destinations. Who made those cars? You might be tempted to say Tesla—and you would be wrong. The automobiles belonged to Cruise (owned by GM with partnerships including Honda, Microsoft, and Walmart) and Waymo (owned by Alphabet, Google's parent company).

It was not just one or two prototype cars; Cruise had 100 driverless cars on the road. They were not in cordoned-off test tracks under ideal conditions; the cars were on busy San Francisco streets. And they were not some futuristic prototypes, but today's cars retrofitted with technologies to understand the shape of things to come. GM was boldly experimenting with Cruise to become a fusion company, aware that its rivals weren't only automakers but also digital companies such as Google (Waymo), Tesla, BYD, Geely, Rivian, Nio, and other startups that are developing new ways to deliver value in transportation and mobility.

Meanwhile, Tesla had started rolling out its Full Self-Driving beta package in November 2022. While the traditional automakers were busy announcing their goals to be all-electric or carbon-neutral, with their expected number of electric vehicles sold in the tens of thousands, Tesla was poised to deliver two million electric cars in 2023.

The number of cars produced, the traditional indicator of industry dominance, still defines how the automobile industry operates. Industrials must shift away from the leadership metrics of the past and embrace metrics that reflect an in-depth understanding of how their products solve customer problems.

Tesla executives get how important the number of cars produced is for Wall Street, but their internal operations are geared toward observing cars as they're driven. With multiple cameras in the automobiles' bodies, Tesla engineers observe every mile their vehicles travel to fine-tune their hardware and software. While Cruise collects data using 100 vehicles, and Waymo from 1,000, Tesla does so from over 2 million cars. Every Tesla is designed to interconnect the physical and digital domains, creating the ability to collect data in motion (fusion force 1).

The company is distinct because, since 2016, every Tesla has had a built-in "shadow mode" that simulates the driving process in parallel with the human driver, even if the car's Autopilot system is not in use.[4] When the algorithm's predictions don't match the driver's behavior, snapshots of the car's cameras, speed, acceleration, and other parameters are recorded and sent to Tesla. Its AI team reviews and analyzes the data to identify human actions that the system should imitate and use as training data for its neural networks. For instance, the team may notice that the system fails to identify road signs obscured by trees and figure out ways for it to get better-quality data.

Intelligent humans and powerful machines learn together (fusion force 2). Tesla's neural network has been improving with data collected over more miles by more cars driving worldwide. CEO Elon Musk put it succinctly in April 2019 at Tesla AI Day: "Essentially every (driver) is training the (neural) network all the time . . . whether Autopilot's on or off, the network is being trained." Tesla has built a supercomputer platform from the ground up for machine learning, called Dojo, and is developing supercomputing capabilities for a range of tasks: training neural networks with data from its fleet of vehicles, auto-labeling training videos from its fleet, and training its neural networks to build a self-driving system. Using real-time multimedia data in this way is beyond the capabilities of most traditional automakers.

What excites strategists is Gen AI's power to transform industrial companies whose applications are stuck in prehistoric architectures. Its most significant impact will be in how industrial applications use multiple types of data to derive deeper insights. What may have been lost in the cacophony around AI is that transformer neural networks that process sequential data efficiently and effectively can be used to build large language models such as GPT-4. Beyond consumer applications such as generating text, images, sounds, computer codes, and videos, they can be applied in industrial applications such as helping vehicles understand complicated intersections and drivable pathways or industrial robots to carry out different tasks.

As Gen AI helps humans become more productive and creative, Tesla's AI models will enhance the efficacy and safety of autonomous driving. Mastery of industry-specific language models will increasingly differentiate the winners from the also-rans.

Traditional automakers, which not so long ago mocked electric vehicles (EVs) as glorified golf carts, were all in on EVs by 2023. The global shift from the industrial combustion engine to battery electric vehicles seems irreversible. Winning in the future calls for seamlessly integrating traditional competencies in the design and manufacturing of automobiles with emerging digital disciplines such as hardware, software, applications, connectivity, telematics, and analytics.

There's greater recognition among the incumbents that automobiles must be rethought and redesigned as cloud-connected computers on wheels. So, automakers must become digital engineering companies with competencies at the intersection of traditional disciplines and digital technologies (fusion force 3). Mercedes-Benz and Volkswagen are committed to developing their operating systems and mastering software competencies. Cruise has prototyped Origin, a zero-emission EV designed to operate without a human driver; it's a reimagination of the automobile without human-centered features like a steering wheel or a sun visor. Waymo, in collaboration with Geely's Zeekr, has prototyped its vision of vehicles without steering wheels, accelerators, or brakes.

The automotive sector also shows the emergent role of the metaverse. BMW, for instance, is using Nvidia's Omniverse platform to build a factory where people and robots work together closely and engineers collaborate in virtual spaces. With information from design and planning tools generating realistic images of the planned factory,

BMW can assess the critical trade-offs it must make in production systems. In addition to factory design, Nvidia's platform allows automakers to evaluate how autonomous vehicles perform on the road by creating simulations of highways or urban streets to test the vehicle's perception systems, decision-making capabilities, and control logic (fusion force 4).

Even so, the sector is at a crossroads. The core product of automobiles is fast becoming a digital industrial product, with powerful systems-on-chip driven by millions of lines of software code. The business processes involved in designing, producing, assembling, and delivering the vehicle are increasingly supported by digital twins and metaverse-driven digital environments. Service delivery, which is progressively personalized, is supported by telematics, cloud connectivity, over-the-air software updates, and timely recommendations.

Importantly, automakers are enmeshed in overlapping ecosystems with traditional and digital companies for complementary capabilities and interoperability. GM is scaling Cruise in partnership with Honda, Microsoft, and Walmart. GM, which developed its Ultium battery and motor with LG Chem, might invite other automobile manufacturers to become partners once it reaches production for deployment at scale. Motional, the joint venture between Hyundai and Aptiv, has partnered with Uber for autonomous rides and delivery. Tesla, which has open-sourced its patents, could invite other automakers to use Dojo to enhance the reliability and safety of autonomous driving systems.

Countless other alliances are being struck as companies try to de-risk their portfolios through partnerships. Automotive ecosystems involve competitive and cooperative relationships. Many automakers have jettisoned legacy practices and become embedded in emerging networks, with many announcing their intent to be part of Tesla's charging network in the United States. Uber exemplifies a fusion company that puts ecosystems front and center. Its ability to coordinate and match riders with drivers in thousands of cities is based on assembling the ecosystem of relevant partners and ensuring that they have real-time data to deliver the services (fusion force 5).

The five fusion forces don't apply only to the automotive sector, which we believe to be the best example today. The forces also operate in farming, agriculture, mining, construction, real estate, health care, transportation, logistics, and other asset-heavy sectors. Every industrial product will become digital. Every industrial company will become a digital industrial company and compete against digital natives. Therefore, every industrial must redesign its strategy and operations by combining humans and machines. Every industrial company must develop a fusion strategy.

Impressive developments will result as traditional engineering disciplines—mechanical, chemical, civil, aerospace, agriculture, and metallurgy—intersect with digital technology. Ask farming executives, and you will hear them speak of precision farming and decision agriculture, with autonomous tractors operating remotely through the cloud, and ecosystems involving traditional players (seeds, fertilizers, and equipment manufacturers) and digital players (satellite providers, farming cloud operators, data modelers, and AI experts). Probe construction executives about the future of building design, and they will discuss self-healing materials, intelligent buildings, and connected windows that optimize comfort and sustainability. Talk to executives in the airline industry, and they will describe data and analytics as being the drivers of sustainable, efficient, and safe flying.

Choose any industry you like, and if you ask executives to sketch out their views on the shifts over the next decade—you will find that they cover the five fusion forces.

From Strategy *Now* to Strategy *Next*

Ultimately, the end game here is to use data-rich insights to create new products, customer experiences, and services. But it's important to note: Fusion strategy is not a push to simply use more technology. We aren't suggesting that you develop an ABCD digital strategy, where A stands for AI, B for blockchain, C for cloud, and D for data.

We aren't telling you to overlay technology on your old business logic, or to selectively leverage some technology for specific objectives within narrowly defined functions.

Rather, fusion strategy builds on the lessons learned from the asset-light sectors and adapts them to the needs of the asset-heavy sectors. It shows the trajectories for exponential growth that were previously impossible without data and AI. It outlines how digital technologies change the competitive landscape, with new companies and competencies unlocking fresh value.

The dynamics of fusion strategy are different. In the past, industrial companies expanded or diversified by acquiring companies that made similar or related products and components. Fusion strategy suggests an alternative: define a software architecture, interlink with other companies, and generate data-driven insights that will boost customer productivity and allow industrials to capture some of the value they have unlocked. Since acquiring and integrating physical assets is often complex and inefficient, industrial companies would do better to interconnect through data-based alliances and partnerships. Doing so will also prove more effective, since the system's scope will change over time as new machines are added and old systems are removed.

Strategy has often focused on what a company can do with its existing resources and capabilities. Industrials have sought product-market extensions and diversification by acquiring physical resources—factories, component manufacturers, distribution warehouses, logistics companies, and so on. These are still relevant, but today they're competitive table stakes.

Over the next decade, differentiation may come from mergers and acquisitions that create the fusion between physical and digital. These are not about making analog products digital with sensors and software, but about adopting the technologies needed to develop next-generation industrial products and systems and to expand the scope of datagraphs and AI proficiency.

Strategic thinking has long been firm-centric. But fusion strategy balances owning assets with developing relationships to access other data-rich assets. Wise CEOs will recognize that fusion strategies are network-centric. The industrials must embed themselves in ecosystems that cut across industry boundaries, with data flowing continually across different machines. Those who see their roles in newly forming digital ecosystems will win.

Our Invitation

This book covers today's best practices in a landscape where incumbents and digital companies compete with diverse levels of reliance on digital technologies. We don't showcase a set of best-in-class companies and ask you to emulate them. Instead, we've drawn lessons from the born-digital companies that compete with datagraphs and algorithms in asset-light settings to derive strategy principles for asset-heavy settings.[5] The road to the fusion future lies ahead, and the scale, scope, and speed of transformation will be challenging for even industrial leaders.

Fusion will not happen only in the United States, where the first wave of digitization started before spreading globally. The next wave will be far-reaching as the industrial worlds embrace next-generation technologies such as the internet of things (IoT), robotics, cloud, AI—and especially Gen AI, vision computing, and others. Industry 4.0, already evident in South Korea and Germany, will be as global as total quality management became late in the twentieth century. With its decade-long digitalization drive, India may be on the threshold of evolving from the world's back office to an advanced manufacturing powerhouse, with digital as the catalyst.

You may be in a company that makes medical instruments for laboratories, intelligent devices for the home, or wearable devices that allow us to monitor our health. Yesterday's speakers delivered high-fidelity sounds; today's are conversational interfaces for voice computing; tomorrow's will be part of spatial computing. Today kitchens are fitted with standard appliances, but tomorrow they will be infused with sensors, and software will communicate their uses, needs, and conditions. This book will help you go beyond merely adding digital features for differentiation and instead see them as ways to observe your products in use. Remotely monitoring home appliances is a start; ensuring they are fixed before breaking down is the future.

Or you may be in an asset-heavy company in the automotive, agriculture and farming, mining, transportation, logistics, or construction sectors. Automation and autonomy require product-in-use data. Farms and mines are more easily instrumented with telemetry than roads, offering opportunities for heavy equipment companies to understand how datagraphs and data network effects operate. Developing a ten-year road map of trucks, tractors, and trailers must be guided by fusion thinking. The strategies described in this book will help you find new ways to unlock value and develop new sources of advantage.

Or you may be qualified as an engineer but feel unable to convince top management to invest in digitizing industrial products. This book will help you develop an investment thesis based on digital twins that feed data to make your products perpetually upgradeable. You will learn the vocabulary that connects digital engineering to business performance.

Or you may have graduated from a business school, where you mastered customer-centricity principles, but you are frustrated with your organization's legacy approach to data, with siloed systems and uncoordinated definitions. This book will help you articulate the need to invest in graph data structures to reach the next generation of customer centricity.

Or you may be in HR, tasked with educating employees about the future. This book will help you understand how datagraphs and AI guide decisions across the company. You will find that the fusion strategies we outline help you identify the attributes of leaders who win in a fusion world.

Or you may be a data scientist, well versed in the latest models and algorithms but find yourself in a company that hasn't fully grasped the implications of how data and AI reshape competition. You can sit with your business colleagues, map your company's position relative to rivals, and develop ways to get richer data to push the frontiers of competition. You will find a framework that connects data architectures to business design in a competitive context that redistributes value.

It doesn't matter what your professional degree or functional title is. The only thing that matters is that you are passionate about the power of digital technologies as a strategy driver and that you believe the industrials can win. You disagree with the experts who say industrial companies are doomed to fail and only born-digital companies will seize the future.

We're with you. We're convinced that today's leaders can win if they recognize and respond to the digitalization of the industrial sector. But you cannot afford to wait: as Amazon's Jeff Bezos put it, "Most decisions should probably be made with somewhere around 70 percent of the information you wish you had. If you wait for 90 percent, in most cases, you're probably being slow."[6]

We invite you to engage with this book today because the time to read, reflect, and respond strategically is *now*. As Mahatma Gandhi said: "The future depends on what you do today." Tomorrow, we fear, may be too late.

CHAPTER 2

Digital Upstarts Vanquished Consumer Giants

O F THE MORE THAN TEN THOUSAND PRODUCTS AMAZON sells every minute, as many as half of the sales are based on personalized recommendations. Its algorithms arrange the products you see when you visit the site, narrowing them down from about 353 million items, using its ability to predict what you may want at that precise moment. It's as if you walked into a store in Diagon Alley with Harry Potter, and the shelves magically rearranged themselves so that the products you're most likely to buy are closest to you—and the rest recede into the background. It would be impossible to do that in a physical store.

Over the last two decades, Amazon has connected people's purchase histories with their browsing data, their viewing data from Prime Video, their listening data from Amazon Music, and so on to create a purchase graph. The company's ability to understand customers extends to voice computing (Alexa), online health care stores (PillPack), physical stores (Whole Foods, Amazon Go), and payment platforms (Amazon Pay). Its algorithms map product-to-product interconnections and use collaborative filtering, incorporating factors such as diversity (how dissimilar items are), serendipity (how surprising the recommended items are), and novelty (how new the recommended items are). As a result of its rich data and elaborate personalization, Amazon's share of the U.S. e-commerce market is more than 40 percent, with its closest rival, Walmart, at only 7 percent.

In May 2021 Google announced its Shopping Graph, which the company described as "a dynamic, AI-enhanced model that understands a constantly changing set of products, sellers, brands, reviews and most importantly, the product information and inventory data we receive from brands and retailers directly—as well as how those attributes relate to one another."[1] It's based on Google's machine-learning algorithms, with real-time data on availability, reviews, colors, and sizes. With over a billion people researching products on Google daily, the company's Shopping Graph connects users to over thirty-five billion listings from millions of merchants.

Google's unparalleled Knowledge Graph interconnects interrelated information to uncover comprehensive insights beyond just retrieving data that best matches the user's search queries and helps users not just to find answers but also to explore and understand related concepts. Combined with Android, voice and image search, Chrome browser extensions, Google Assistant, Gmail, Photos, Maps, Google Cloud, Google Pay, YouTube, and other services, Knowledge Graph helps position the company to meet Amazon's challenge. One piece that Google needs to add is a fulfillment engine like the one Amazon built to deliver products. However, instead of building their own, Google has deepened its partnership with Shopify, the Canadian upstart. It lets the latter's 4.5 million merchants offer listings across Google, provides the algorithms that connect shoppers and consumers, and allows the merchants on Shopify to handle the logistics.

The shopping wars are now fought with a new weapon: data. Not just anything under the umbrella of big data, but rather smart data that allows leaders to construct distinctive datagraphs that form the basis of strategy and how they compete.[2]

Drawing on Datagraphs for Strategy

In April 2020 China officially recognized data as a new factor of production, which reflects how information is changing business models, industry boundaries, and market structures worldwide.[3] Yet data in business is often taken for granted, used for mundane purposes, and poorly connected to strategy. Companies drowning in data lakes and burying data in warehouses don't regard it as crucial; other parameters take precedence. Not all executives relate to the strategic value of data. They sense that it's a source of value, but at the same time they feel that it's a source of risk, a regulatory constraint, and that there are sensitivities in how it can be used. Some are proud of their intuitive decision-making capabilities, seeing little need for data-driven insights, while many don't trust data when making tough calls.

The recent development of digital tools means it's easier to store vast amounts of data in the cloud and study them. Traditionally, companies have relied on *systems of record*, gathering data on who bought what, how much, when, and at what price. They have used those records for mundane purposes such as maintenance or service warranties. The data is usually stored in databases that are maintained separately by their manufacturing, marketing, sales, and accounting functions.

In the early 2000s, with the growth of the internet, and later in the 2010s, with the explosion of smartphones, companies began using *systems of engagement* to periodically connect with customers through email, websites, mobile apps, and social media such as Facebook pages, X/Twitter feeds, TikTok videos, and Instagram accounts. Doing so enabled companies to develop budding customer relationships even though only some buyers were interested in communicating with or interacting with sellers. Systems of engagement marked an improvement over systems of record, so companies assumed they were doing all they could with data.

Over the past decade, a few companies have started collecting real-time data from everything they sell by embedding sensors, connectivity devices, and software in it. These technologies allow organizations to track products as consumers use them. Enterprises can gather product-in-use data on each unit, aggregate it for all products and buyers, and analyze the data, which can be in structured or unstructured forms such as text, images, videos, and sounds. By systematically tracking real-time data, companies like Amazon and Google have used it to win by developing datagraphs.

Datagraphs, a construct we developed a few years back and use in our teaching and consulting work, capture the relationships, links, and interrelationships between a company and its customers through product-in-use data. The concept is inspired by social networks and graph theory, where a *social graph* is defined as a representation of the interconnections between individuals, who are depicted as nodes, and the relationships between them—friends, colleagues, supervisors, and so on—which are depicted as links.[4] The word *graph* refers to the nature of the linkages, which identify the critical characters in the network, such as the hubs, the connectors, and the influencers.

The concept can be traced to the work of the social psychologist Stanley Milgram on "small worlds" and the theory that each of us is, on average, six or fewer social connections away from each other. (The idea has been popularized as "six degrees of separation," a term that Milgram did not use.) Social network theory posits that the relationships and ties between the actors in a network (that is, us) matter significantly. This perspective has proven to be a valuable lens for analyzing the structures and dynamics of organizations, industries, markets, and societies.

In the same way, the ties that a company's datagraphs display are more critical than its data on individual customers, products, features, and their uses. That assertion stands the test of logic: when different pieces of data can be connected, especially in real time, they can all be understood at a deeper level than in isolation. The use of static data inevitably ends with companies' developing systems of record or systems of engagement, which can provide, at best, standard heuristics. By tracking product-in-use data in real time, companies can create datagraphs that will help them offer personalized prescriptions that go beyond the standard responses that customers often find unsatisfactory.

Unlike data at rest—static data such as age, sex, or geography—datagraphs are dynamic representations. They constantly change because they're based on real-time inputs and reflect what data scientists call data in motion, which refers to the stream of data moving through any network.

Every datagraph has three characteristics—*scale, scope,* and *speed.* Scale is represented by the number of nodes or data points a company tracks. Scope is a function of how many attributes it monitors at each node. Speed shows how fast and frequently the organization collects data.

A datagraph becomes more valuable as its scale rises, its scope expands, and the speed of its data collection increases. The richer the datagraph, the better the opportunities to impact the moments that matter for customers, and the more comprehensive a company's strategy choices become. Companies can develop new datagraphs based on new offerings or make their existing datagraphs richer through alliances and partnerships, such as the one Google struck to deepen its link with Shopify.[5]

Companies can also expand the scale, scope, and speed of their datagraphs through acquisitions. Since Microsoft took it over in 2015, LinkedIn, whose professional graph captures how around eight hundred million professionals work in more than fifty million companies, has grown in stature. Imagine the possibilities. Here is how Microsoft's CEO, Satya Nadella, vividly described the opportunity:

How people find jobs, build skills, sell, market, and get work done, and, ultimately, find success requires a connected professional world. It requires a vibrant network that combines a professional's information in LinkedIn's public network with the information in Office 365 and Dynamics. This combination will make it possible for new experiences such as a LinkedIn newsfeed that serves up articles based on the project you're working on, and Office suggesting an expert to connect with via LinkedIn to help with a task you're trying to complete . . ."[6]

The professional graph is richer and more comprehensive than individual HR organizations could ever assemble and put to use. By 2023, with Gen AI coming of age, LinkedIn, Microsoft 365, and Microsoft Teams are collectively becoming a treasure trove of data, architected with Microsoft Graph as the foundation.[7]

Several digitals have used datagraphs (although they don't all use our term; some use a more general term, *knowledge graph*, which should be distinguished from Google's capitalized Knowledge Graph) to become leaders in consumer markets. The more successful datagraphs—such as Amazon's purchase graph, Google's search graph, Facebook's social graph, Netflix's movie graph, Spotify's music graph, Airbnb's travel graph, Uber's mobility graph, and LinkedIn's professional graph—have been developed by digital companies whose products and services consumers use every day. These leaders use datagraphs and proprietary AI and business algorithms to derive real-time insights to outcompete rivals on every front, from personalized customer recommendations, product creation, and service delivery to marketing, advertising, and sales.

The Power of Data Network Effects

The practice of successfully building datagraphs starts with capturing, parsing, and analyzing product-in-use data, a process that is helped by data network effects. Data network effects are generated when users actively (by using a product or service) or passively (by offering feedback) provide data that makes a product or service more valuable for other users. For example, each of the 1.2 trillion searches that people make on Google annually helps the company enrich its Knowledge Graph, refine its search engine, increase the quality of searches for other users, and improve Bard, Google's version of a Gen AI–based assistant.[8]

The same logic applies to Spotify, Netflix, and Airbnb: every consumer interaction with a song, a movie, or a destination, respectively, provides valuable data that helps the digital giants deliver better experiences to other consumers. When a business aggregates and analyzes data using machine learning algorithms, it can learn how to personalize the value for everyone in the network based on collective information. The more interactions companies foster, the greater the data network effects.

Data network effects are quite different from direct network effects, which accrue to a company when adding a new user increases the value of the offering for all the other users. That phenomenon gained popularity in the early internet era, with the first digital firms using them to advance in businesses such as social networking, email, and messaging. Companies can also benefit from indirect network effects, triggered when a greater base of users catalyzes the development of a more significant number of complementary products and services. For example, a rise in the sale of Android devices incentivizes software developers to write more apps for Google Play, Google's app store, which makes the operating system more attractive to potential buyers and developers.

Unlike direct and indirect network effects, data network effects don't require companies to add more users to enhance their networks' value. Even if no new users join and no one leaves, the value of data network effects increases because of the continual engagement of users and their contribution to product-in-use data (see figure 2-1).

The science behind a datagraph predates digitalization. Instead of using lines to connect points and trace a graph, datagraphs connect entities to other entities through structured and unstructured data,

FIGURE 2-1

Distinguishing data network effects from direct and indirect network effects

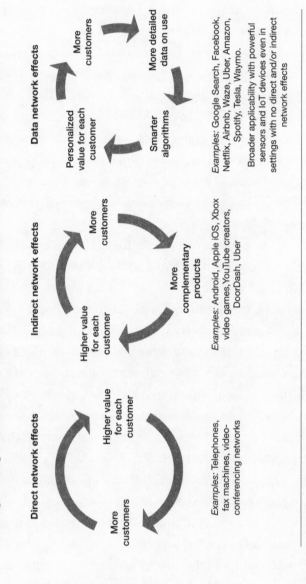

Direct network effects

Higher value for each customer

More customers

Examples: Telephones, fax machines, video-conferencing networks

Indirect network effects

Higher value for each customer

More customers

More complementary products

Examples: Android, Apple iOS, Xbox video games, YouTube creators, DoorDash, Uber

Data network effects

Personalized value for each customer

More customers

More detailed data on use

Smarter algorithms

Examples: Google Search, Facebook, Netflix, Airbnb, Waze, Uber, Amazon, Spotify, Tesla, Waymo.

Broader applicability with powerful sensors and IoT devices even in settings with no direct and/or indirect network effects schema markup, or code conveying their meaning. It isn't possible to draw a schematic of a datagraph manually; digital technologies are necessary to gather data in real time on the millions of units of each of a company's products that consumers worldwide are using at any point in time, and to draw, interpret, and analyze the resulting datagraphs with powerful algorithms. Companies need computing power, AI, and ML to create datagraphs, study them, and generate actionable insights, which is why the use of datagraphs to develop strategy has become possible only in the last five years.

How Datagraph Leaders Win

The datagraph pioneers collect and analyze product-in-use data and quickly incorporate the learnings to improve their offerings. They constantly refine the classification and labeling of data, searching for relationships between categories so that their AI can make personalized recommendations. They continually refine their algorithms such that recommendations are based on the most current and relevant data, which helps improve customer engagement, satisfaction, and loyalty. The digitals get ahead and stay there because they use datagraphs to trigger three forces that continuously reinforce their ability to create and capture value, as table 2-1 shows.

They learn at scale and speed

Datagraphs capture how individuals live, work, play, learn, listen, socialize, watch, transact, travel, spend, and any other activity that is associated with a business. Digitalization has made these actions observable and codifiable at scale in real time. For instance, Meta's portfolio of datagraphs is based on data from over three billion users on seven platforms—Facebook, Messenger, WhatsApp, Instagram, Oculus, the company's metaverse, and Threads.

TABLE 2-1

How digitals leverage network effects in direct-to-consumer markets

Datagraph leader	Direct network effects	Indirect network effects	Data network effects	Description of datagraph
Airbnb	No	Yes	Yes	Travel graph
Amazon	No	Yes	Yes	Purchase graph
American Express	No	Yes	Yes	Spend graph
Coursera	No	Yes	Yes	Skills graph
Facebook	Yes	Yes	Yes	Social graph
Google	No	Yes	Yes	Search graph
LinkedIn	Yes	Yes	Yes	Professional graph
Netflix	No	Yes	Yes	Movie graph
Stitch Fix	No	Yes	Yes	Style graph
Spotify	No	Yes	Yes	Music graph
Twitter	Yes	Yes	Yes	Influence graph

Note: We created the descriptions of the datagraphs to highlight the domain area that the different companies represent; they are not necessarily used within these companies.

Meta tracks what each user is doing; who they're befriending, unfriending, or messaging; where they're traveling; what brands they're talking about; what movies they're watching; and what music they're listening to. It has mastered the science of collecting user data in real time on the billions of interactions between its members and log-ons, click-throughs, visit durations, page views, and searches.

Doing so allows the digital giant to run trials, experiments, and A/B tests, ensuring its members spend time on its offerings. For instance, before Facebook shows someone a post or an ad, it sorts through a large inventory and narrows the choice to a set of around five hundred options the user is likely to engage with, based on past patterns. Then, its proprietary neural network ranks them before showing them to the user across several media, such as its text, audio, and video platforms. This allows Facebook to ensure that users will engage with that content virtually, and when they do so, it quickly increases the scale of the company's social graph.

They expand scope and dynamically enrich their offerings

Most datagraph leaders organize the data they collect in machine-readable graph form. For example, Airbnb's travel graph is based on its inventory of about seven million homes, tagged by entities (cities, landmarks, events, etc.) and their relationships (best time to visit, famous churches, best shows, etc.). As consumers use Airbnb's curated experiences and tag locations on social media, the digital firm tracks the room each individual rented, the places of interest they visited, where they dined, the shows they watched, and so on.

This tracking enables Airbnb to link all the offerings each individual consumes, aggregate the data across customers, group them based on the similarity of products, and provide future visitors with personalized recommendations about not just the type of house to rent but also the best places for dinner or the best times to visit attractions. The firm's ability to expand the scope of its offerings allows it to serve customers better than a traditional hotel, where guest data can be found in each departmental silo (e.g., reservations will have data on bookings, concierge services will have data on day trips and restaurants, and the spa will have data on the services used).

Most digital companies have taken their cue from Google's Knowledge Graph. We've all done research in physical libraries, where information is stored in independent data silos. However, Google isn't a virtual library; it has built a more interconnected system over the last twenty years, organizing all the facts it has gathered into distinct and independent elements. Each offers different kinds of information but connects to many other factors. When Google introduced its datagraph, it had indexed more than 500 million entities, more than 3.5 billion facts about them, and countless interrelationships. Since then, the scale and scope of Google's Knowledge Graph, and the underlying database, have only grown.

Google's advantage lies in the datasets it has created, which capture all the relationships between entities in ways that help its algorithms understand the context of each search. For instance, when a user enters the word "jaguar" in Google's search bar, are they searching for the South American animal, the British automobile, or the American football team? At first, Google's algorithms couldn't tell the difference. Based on past patterns and user behavior, the digital has developed condition-based rules predicting one meaning over another. For instance, if a user has searched for animals recently, chances are that they're looking to know more about the animal than the automobile or the football team.

To arrive at that conclusion, Google has organized and linked all its databases in a graph-based architecture. The graph-based structure helps it respond to even orally expressed queries such as, "Hey Google, book two tickets to the Roman Forum and the Colosseum for next Wednesday and charge it to Google Pay." Because the underlying knowledge is represented as a graph, the algorithm understands what the user is asking; it knows the "Roman Forum" and the "Colosseum" are attractions in Rome, next Wednesday is April 19, to "book" means to buy tickets, and to "charge" means to use a stored credit card, as opposed to other meanings of those words.

As consumers interact and meanings change, the underlying Knowledge Graph gets refined and updated to represent the relationships. Consider a search query by a mountaineer who has hiked Mount Adams and would like to climb Mount Fuji next. They may ask, "What should I do to prepare differently for Mount Fuji than Mount Adams?" The user will need to conduct multiple searches to get an answer to this query. By 2023 Google provided more-pertinent answers because of interlinkages across different databases and seamless translation across languages. Only a glimpse of this functionality can be currently seen with Bard. Still, Gen AI is poised to enrich the offerings of digital companies as they build conversational interfaces that allow customers to interact using words, images, numbers, and voice.

Analog companies have only records of individual products purchased across different owners in different data formats. It's tough for them to determine how consumers purchase across product or business categories. This weakness has created opportunities for the digitals to carve out niches by developing a system that logically connects the meaning across different entities, allowing them to see patterns of preference across products; use them to penetrate markets by finding cracks; and, over time, widen those niches to dominate the market.

Because this strategy depends on the scale and scope of datagraphs, incumbents would do well to follow the cybersecurity truism: defenders think in lists, attackers think in graphs. The latter always win because while defenders develop a defense for an attack in isolation, attackers, knowing that digital systems are interconnected, identify the most vulnerable nodes for penetrating, wresting control of, and gaining access to the entire network. In the same way, datagraphs are dynamic networks of interconnections in graph form that reveal more and better opportunities.

They develop distinctive business algorithms to win

Datagraphs can be converted into value through business algorithms, which are rules for creating and capturing value. The leaders' differentiation stems from the datagraphs they create and the business algorithms they develop to generate results. The business algorithms help develop four kinds of analyses—descriptive analysis ("What happened?"), diagnostic analysis ("Why did it happen?"), predictive analysis ("What could happen?"), and prescriptive analytics ("What should happen?")—and link them together in powerful ways to generate competitive advantage.

Consider, for instance, Netflix, whose subscribers, unlike Facebook and LinkedIn users, aren't connected to one another. Even so, the streaming service infers consumer preferences by tracking everything a viewer watches on its platform in real time to construct a movie graph for that individual. It doesn't sell customer data, but Netflix wrings more value from product-in-use data than any of its rivals in the entertainment industry.

The company has detailed data on every movie or show each viewer is watching: the day, time, and zip code where it is being watched; on what kind of screen (cell phone, tablet, computer, or TV); when the viewer pauses, fast-forwards, or rewinds; and when the consumer starts and stops watching. In addition, it collects granular data into what led someone to watch a particular movie or show in the first place, in the form of detailed records of how they navigated the menus and what they clicked on.

Based on all that data, Netflix algorithmically customizes its home screen—and updates it continuously—for every subscriber and recommends what a consumer may like to watch at any moment. In 2001 only 2 percent of Netflix's recommendations were chosen by its 456,000 users. By 2020 nearly 80 percent of viewers were choosing one of its recommendations on their home screens rather than searching for content, and Netflix had more than 200 million subscribers.

In addition to product-in-use data, Netflix has tagged all its content by genre, language, actor, director, and other attributes. User ratings, which are simple thumbs-ups or -downs, and users' revealed preferences serve as inputs for Netflix's proprietary algorithms, creating the consideration set for each viewer. For example, if a subscriber watched a TV serial yesterday, should it be weighed twice as much or ten times as much as something they watched a month ago? How should the algorithm factor in that the viewer stopped watching some shows after ten minutes, binge-watched others over a weekend, and raced through some series immediately after their release? These attributes matter for all users but differently for each of them.

Netflix's edge lies in using its datagraphs to train its AI to create thousands of virtual taste communities, or people who watch the same kinds of things that you watch. These communities are key to curating and personalizing recommendations for each subscriber.

They help Netflix in its quest to win what it calls the *moment of truth*—a two-minute window in which a viewer decides whether to watch something on Netflix. If the viewer doesn't go with one of its recommendations, the company has lost the battle to one of the other services, such as Apple TV, Max, Hulu, Disney+, Peacock, cable on demand, or regular old TV. In 2015 Netflix estimated that it had saved over $1 billion because its personalized recommendation engine had prevented people from canceling their subscriptions.

The company's datagraph even guides its content development strategy. Because Netflix can predict what its viewers will watch, it uses those proprietary insights to produce movies and serials that are more likely to succeed. Hollywood's studios mostly create films based on gut instinct and past box office results, and TV networks base their programming and advertising rates on Nielsen viewer ratings. These predigital pointers are primitive and poorly suited to customization. Netflix's datagraph has allowed it to change the rules, from eliminating pilot episodes—Netflix outbid HBO for the rights to produce *House of Cards* and acquired the rights to create *The Crown* based on data and algorithms—to encouraging binge-watching by dropping an entire set of episodes at the same time.

As Netflix develops its ad-supported tier of subscriptions, it must expand the scale, scope, and speed of its datagraphs to focus on specific types of advertisements that offer value to advertisers and minimize customer irritations and frustrations. Its decision to work with Microsoft—a leader in datagraphs even before its recent push into AI—could introduce a new advertising powerhouse that will rival Google and Meta.

Strategists must remember that the power of business algorithms differentiates the winners from the losers in the digital world: Facebook from Myspace, Google from AltaVista, Spotify from Pandora, and Amazon from every other retailer. A business algorithm is a proprietary reasoning and inference engine that interlinks descriptive, diagnostic, predictive, and prescriptive analyses. These types of analysis shouldn't be conducted independently; leaders use business algorithms to do all four simultaneously in an overarching framework, drawing on a rich datagraph of interrelationships and dependencies.

Datagraphs Get Fueled by Generative AI

Gen AI, the next inflection point in the evolution of AI, can generate new content in unstructured forms from foundation models such as GPT-4, PaLM, Stable Diffusion, and DALL-E 2. These models have captured the imagination of people and professionals because they can be used to create text, audio, images, animations, and movies without much programming.

Gen AI chatbots leverage foundation models and extensive neural networks trained on large, diverse, quantitative, qualitative, and unstructured datasets, enabling various tasks. Unlike narrow AI, which performs single tasks like predicting customer churn or optimizing production runs, Gen AI models are versatile and capable of tasks such as summarizing technical reports, developing new product ideas, providing varied recipes, and doing complex programming.

The core ideas are captured by the three letters in GPT: *generative, pretrained,* and *transformer.* A transformer is an artificial neural network trained using deep learning, which alludes to the many layers within a neural network. GPT models require large investments to develop because of the substantial computational resources needed to train them and the human effort required to refine them. As a result, GPT models have been designed primarily by a few tech giants, such as Microsoft (with OpenAI), Google, Meta, and Nvidia. Others are developing applications atop foundation models for copy editing, writing assistants, product designs, media and advertising, art, and software code generation.

Gen AI models generate datagraphs on steroids to offer much richer insights. Unsurprisingly, the datagraph leaders are racing to incorporate the technology to make their graphs more powerful. For instance, Google and Microsoft are locked in a new search war using Gen AI. With a multibillion-dollar equity investment in OpenAI, Microsoft is rearchitecting its Bing search engine to challenge Google's approach to monetizing search through advertising. Meanwhile, Google is supercharging its search with Bard. Without Gen AI, a search query on Google—say, "Which is better for a family with kids under three years old and a dog, Bryce Canyon or the Grand Canyon?"—would result in a set of links that the user would have to peruse before making a decision. Using Gen AI results in a response (albeit with links) that can be further queried with the context carried forward, as would happen in everyday conversations. Google's next move will be to leverage DeepMind, the Alphabet-owned company that created the AI program that defeated the world's Go champion, to build on its decade-long investments in AI.

The shopping wars, too, are being fought with Gen AI. Google has built a Gen AI shopping experience on top of its Shopping Graph—with about 1.8 billion of its 35 billion product listings refreshed every hour—based on real-time data on products, reviews, and inventory levels. Amazon is using Gen AI to summarize customer reviews so that buyers do not have to read all the comments to get a sense of positive and negative feedback.

Meta, meanwhile, is creating Gen AI–infused tools to help advertisers create ads calibrated to appeal to different individuals. At the same time, advertising firm WPP has formed links with Nvidia to push the frontier of customized advertising.[9] Google and the Microsoft-Netflix partnership will also intensify advertising wars with Gen AI.

Spotify has debuted DJ, an AI-powered disc jockey, which combines its mastery over the music graph with Gen AI in the form of a personalized guide that knows an individual's music taste and refreshes their music lineup accordingly. And Airbnb is integrating ChatGPT into its platform and has promised a reinvented travel experience with Gen AI at its core. More powerful innovations are likely as Gen AI's evolution transforms the use of datagraphs.

The Road to Industrial Datagraphs

The digitals have used datagraphs and AI to design business models that have dislodged many of the leaders in consumer markets. It's also becoming evident that only companies that create distinctive datagraphs and develop differentiated business algorithms can compete and win in a data-driven world. Because many of the incumbents in consumer industries didn't recognize the transformative power of data, datagraphs, and algorithms, the digitals quickly surpassed them.

It's logical to ask if the digitals can use datagraphs and algorithms to develop strategies to take on the industrials, which currently generate value from proprietary technologies, plant and machinery, and infrastructure. If the digitals can—and there's no reason they cannot—the industrials must learn to take them on. In the next chapter, we show how industrials can survive, and even thrive, in a digital world by learning to develop industrial datagraphs.

CHAPTER 3

Industrial Giants Are Fighting Back

THE INDUSTRIAL COMPANIES AREN'T STANDING BY IDLY AS digital shifts threaten their businesses. Companies such as ABB, Caterpillar, Emerson Electric Co., Foxconn, GM, Honeywell, John Deere, Rolls-Royce, and Siemens recognize the possibility of being disrupted by digital upstarts. They've seen their asset-light counterparts misjudge the threat and have invested time and money in digitalizing their processes and migrating digital operations to the cloud.

Yet those steps won't be enough. The industrials' focus must immediately shift to digitalizing the core of their businesses, namely their products. This entails redesigning industrial machines—such as construction equipment, tractors, electrical grids, and automobiles—to be digital-first. The modern artifacts of the industrial age must be designed for real-time observation, remote fine-tuning, and algorithmic optimization. A fundamental rethinking of product design will be essential for the industrials to counter the digital challenge.

All industrial products will become digital sooner than companies think. They must be infused with the functionality to transmit data while in use at different customer locations. That's an essential cata-lyst for the shift to Industry 4.0, the fourth industrial revolution.[1] This shift is strategic and disruptive because it invites born-digital compa-nies to enter industrial sectors with new competencies and compels leaders in industrial companies to learn from what happened in the asset-light sectors.

Some CEOs have acted to position their companies for the fusion future. Since 2020 Deere's CEO, John May, has been shaping its digi-tal industrial strategy by combining, as the company put it, "smart industrial strategy, which accelerates the integration of advanced technology, with Deere's legacy of manufacturing excellence."[2] Deere aims to deliver intelligent, connected machines and applications in agriculture and construction to unlock value across the customer's operations. Its tech stack includes hardware, software, guidance sys-tems, connectivity, and automation with enhanced machine IQ and autonomy. We see Deere's tech stack as a strategy stack that reflects its approach to becoming a smart industrial company.

Honeywell's previous CEO, Darius Adamczyk, a trained computer engineer, infused software into the company's core, and its new CEO, Vimal Kapur, is well versed in driving digital transformation. "We had to have the courage to disrupt what we were doing and become much more of a software company," Adamczyk told us in an interview. By using software competency as the driver, Honeywell is trying to un-lock customer value and boost operating efficiency. It has even taken a majority stake in Quantinuum, a company that develops quantum machine learning for industrial settings, which could accelerate Hon-eywell's digital transformation.

Similarly, in 2021 Herbert Diess, then Volkswagen's chairperson, remarked in Wolfsburg, Germany: "Data and electricity are driv-ing us now. We are improving the charging experience for our elec-tric vehicles. We are providing over-the-air software updates . . . and communicating directly with our customers. Volkswagen enjoys one of the best starting positions in the New Auto competition. We must change from a collection of valuable brands to a digital company reliably operating millions of mobility devices worldwide." Oliver Blume, the company's new CEO, is sticking to the New Auto road map, part of which is a bold move to build a unified technology and software platform, including a new vehicle operating system, a cloud platform, and a new vehicle architecture for all its brands.[3]

Agriculture machinery, buildings and materials, aerospace, and automobiles—different sectors and differing legacies, but with the same challenges and opportunities to reimagine their role and relevance as the digital and the physical fuse together—big iron and big data, steel and silicon, as well as physical and digital infrastructure with data links between machines and the cloud. What should legacy companies do when such interconnections and interlinkages emerge? The fusion future is in front of these companies; what they do today will define whether they will succeed tomorrow.

Those four sectors aren't the only ones caught by the digital innovation, disruption, and transformation tsunami. But they help illustrate the shifts underway and should serve as a call to the senior leaders in every industrial company to think through their strategy options. The starting point, naturally, must be industrial datagraphs.

The Distinctiveness of Industrial Datagraphs

Datagraphs in the consumer and industrial sectors are based on product-in-use data but differ in many ways. Asset-heavy companies must recognize the distinctions between the two types of datagraphs before creating, constructing, and acting on them.

To start, consumer datagraphs are based on a limited number of attributes; for example, did a consumer like an advertisement and accept the discount it offered? These insights are easy to track from afar with simple protocols. By contrast, industrial datagraphs are based on several complex attributes of machines' performance in the field. Capturing data on how automobiles autonomously navigate difficult roads in severe winter conditions and how tractors perform on farms during the sowing season differs from recording data on consumers' music and movie preferences.

Industrial datagraphs may be based on smaller volumes of data than consumer datagraphs, but they're likely to be multimodal, spanning numbers, text, 3D images, and voice interactions. Industrial companies can collect many types of data in real time, such as images of defects, the sounds of machines, and video feeds of autonomous processes.

Developing consumer datagraphs is relatively easy to justify due to their scale and the widespread deployment of smartphones. However, industrial datagraphs require compelling investment theses that link the richness of data to business outcomes.

Knowingly or unknowingly, consumers often give digital-born companies access to personal data. But industrial companies must first seek permission to access, collect, and analyze product-in-use data that legally belongs to the customer. This often requires creating formal contracts and offering incentives to customers for sharing data. Companies must earn the trust of their customers to become the custodian of their data, and keep that trust by providing value in ways that customers cannot achieve on their own.

Industrial datagraphs also involve mission-critical activities. When Amazon fails to deliver a product on time, it can be inconvenient for the customer; when Netflix recommends an uninspiring show, it's irritating. However, when an aircraft engine malfunctions or an autonomous automobile doesn't interpret the road conditions accurately, it will have fatal consequences. The technology infrastructure, accuracy of data, and analytical capabilities required for industrial datagraphs have to be far more robust and powerful than those for consumer datagraphs due to the higher risks involved.

The benefits of industrial datagraphs can be quantified using financial figures, while consumer datagraphs will likely have only indirect impacts. For example, an aircraft engine manufacturer can quantify the impact on the customer's profits due to the reliability and uptime of aircraft engines. At the same time, consumer companies can only indirectly measure effects through metrics like consumer churn or engagement.

Finally, consumer datagraphs can be monetized through advertising or subscriptions, but industrial datagraphs require different approaches. In most cases, they can't be subsidized through advertisements and can only be monetized by delivering value to customers using data-driven insights and tailored recommendations.

Industrial Datagraphs and Generative AI: The Force Multiplier

Fusion strategy builds on industrial datagraphs and, of course, AI. The industrials have, for decades, been at the forefront of using AI in areas as diverse as oil exploration, airline route planning, traffic routing, cybersecurity, and risk management. Those applications have been proprietary, carried out with minimal sharing within or across industries.

Industrial companies now face a Gen AI moment. While the headlines focus on Gen AI's ability to author essays, write poems, and create images, melodies, and movies, its real benefit will be its ability to transform business logic, create new sources of competitive advantage, and render traditional competencies obsolete. Gen AI isn't just about incremental productivity improvements; it will create new forms of economic value. In the process, it will reshape the nature of competitive interactions in industries and ecosystems. Companies that fail to recognize this will have to forgo opportunities and face existential risks.

The internet allowed companies to create e-commerce channels, while smartphones enabled m-commerce. Those two innovations predominantly influenced consumer settings. When it comes to how Gen AI will likely impact industrial companies, it is tailor-made to transform the logic of competition in industrial businesses. The technology is able to, among other things, generate complex designs, extract insights and trends from multimodal data, predict and respond proactively to changing conditions, and handle ambiguous and incomplete data. Gen AI can answer complex questions and solve nonlinear problems accurately and quickly when trained with appropriate, context-specific data. We agree with McKinsey's analysis that the areas where Gen AI will have the most impact in the next eighteen months will be functions and sectors that are asset-heavy and information-rich.[4]

For example, Bloomberg released a new Gen AI model in March 2023, BloombergGPT.[5] Unlike GPT models from OpenAI and others, this large language model has been trained on a wide range of financial data to support diverse natural language processing tasks in the financial industry. In essence, Bloomberg is positioning the technology to create a collaborator for every financial professional. Similarly, Sal Khan, founder of the online education platform Khan Academy, is leveraging Gen AI to create a personalized tutor, Khanmigo, for the platform's students.[6]

Specialized industry-specific models will accelerate the role of Gen AI in transforming the industrial sector. Since this innovation is in its infancy, every company should experiment with this technology and put relevant guardrails in place to ensure the output is trustworthy. Figure 3-1 is a Gen AI architecture schematic with distinct but interconnected tech stacks in industrial sectors. As this architecture evolves, datagraphs and Gen AI will become the combinatory force driving and shaping fusion strategy.

How Industrial Leaders Should Leverage Datagraphs and Gen AI

Industrials must follow three rules to incorporate datagraphs and AI into their strategies and gain a competitive advantage.

1. Engineer data network effects with tripartite twins

Industrial companies typically use one or more of three types of digital twins. A *product twin* represents the product in a virtual environment during the design and development stage (product as

FIGURE 3-1

How a generative tech stack could impact industrial sectors

	Automobiles	Farming	Construction	Buildings
Company-specific models and plug-ins	GM Mercedes-Benz Waymo Tesla	John Deere Bayer Case IH	Caterpillar ABB John Deere	Honeywell Siemens Bechtel
Domain-specific, vertical-industry GPTs	Automobiles	Farming	Construction	Buildings
Cloud platforms (compute hardware exposed to cloud developers)	Amazon Web Service, Oracle, Salesforce, Microsoft Azure, IBM			
Compute hardware (specialized chips for model training)	Nvidia, Google, AMD, Intel, TSMC, IBM			

designed). A *process twin* is a digital representation of the end-to-end manufacturing process, including the role of suppliers and distributors (product as manufactured). And a more recent version, the *performance twin*, digitally represents the product in use to track and collect data on the factors that impact how the product performs in the field (product as deployed).

Often, industrials use digital twins in separate functions, delegating product twins to R&D units and design groups, assigning process twins to supply chain and operations teams, and leaving performance twins to the marketing and service functions. The benefits accrue along narrowly defined metrics if the twins are proposed, funded, and operated independently with boundaries. Industrial data network effects are created by linking the three digital twins: design, manufacturing, and deployment. We refer to this as a *tripartite digital twin*, or a tripartite twin for short (see table 3-1).

Tripartite twins can trace field data back to specific parts, production lines, tier 1 suppliers, and their suppliers. The twin promises to unlock value in the industrial sectors if crucial elements are linked seamlessly from end to end. Combining product and process twins yields significant efficiency benefits, realized at one point. But these

TABLE 3-1

Tripartite digital twins

Distinguishing characteristics	Product twin (as designed)	Process twin (as manufactured)	Performance twin (as deployed)
Vision	To represent the product in a virtual environment during the design and development stage	To represent the end-to-end process of manufacturing	To represent the product-as-deployed to track and collect data on how the product performs in the field
Functional responsibility	Product designers	Manufacturing and supply chain executives	Marketing personnel and service engineers with dealers and partners
Benefits	Trade-offs in using the best configurations of components and subsystems to design the best product	Fine-tuning manufacturing to achieve the best levels of operating efficiency	Track and collect detailed performance data in the field as an input into generating data network effects

two do not create data network effects, which happens only when performance twins are incorporated. A continuous flow of data from the field is necessary to realize its full potential.

Imagine a control center where a manufacturer monitors the performance of all its machines across multiple monitors. This helps executives understand how, when, and where machines operate at their target functioning levels, where they fail, and how long it takes to get them back online. With tripartite twins, the root cause analysis can be carried out continually in the background, supported by graph databases to identify alternative mechanisms to intervene for different customers.

The benefits of tripartite twins become apparent in the example of an accident involving a Tesla car. With the tripartite twin in place,

Tesla pulls up product data as it was designed; process data such as the line, the robots, and the humans who built the car; and relevant performance data such as speed, travel direction, seat belt status, weather, and whether the car was human-driven or the Autopilot system was engaged. Using its tripartite twin, the company links crash-related data to data on all the other Tesla crashes in the past—before emergency vehicles even reach the accident scene—and starts generating hypotheses about the factors that may have caused the latest accident. As teams study such data at scale and speed, they can develop new ways to minimize, if not eliminate, failure. In contrast, many traditional automakers have data only on design and manufacture, which is maintained in functional silos. They do not even collect data on use, thereby limiting their ability to get to the root cause of auto accidents and rendering them unable to generate new approaches to improvements.

When the tripartite twins are designed for seamless dataflows, Gen AI systems can identify plausible reasons for catastrophic failures, such as accidents or minor incidents that, when left unattended, could lead to significant problems later. Developments from technology companies such as Nvidia, C3.ai, PTC, and Siemens offer ways for industrial companies to unify the three disparate twins into a common framework as a precursor to applying and leveraging Gen AI. Table 3-2 summarizes how industrial datagraphs could reshape competition in industrial settings.

It's routine for companies to gather data on consumer behavior with apps and cookies. Still, the industrial world is just starting to explore the possibilities of combining data from multiple sources. Rolls-Royce, for example, has created its R^2 Data Labs to analyze aircraft engine data to improve the services it offers to commercial airlines.[7] Its competitive edge over other engine manufacturers relies on its ability to analyze data at the highest volume, variety, and velocity. Maintaining industrial data leadership requires harnessing tripartite twins and data network effects.

TABLE 3-2

How datagraphs could reshape industrial competition

Industrial sector	Key players that reshape competition using datagraphs
Agriculture and farming	John Deere, Bayer (Monsanto + the Climate Corporation), Case IH, Dow
Personal mobility	Uber, Waze (Google), Didi, Ola, Grab
Automotive mobility	Tesla, Waymo (Google), auto incumbents (GM, Ford, Mercedes-Benz, BMW, Toyota, Hyundai, and others), Continental, Bosch, Firestone
Commercial building operations	Honeywell, Rockwell Automation, Siemens
Airline and aircraft operations	GE, Rolls-Royce, Boeing, Airbus, other Tier 1 suppliers
Oil and gas, energy	Oil majors, Schlumberger, Hughes, Emerson Electric Co., Halliburton
Commercial logistics	UPS, FedEx, DHL, Norfolk Southern, BNSF, CSX
Personalized health	Big Pharma, CVS, Blue Cross Blue Shield, health care providers, Apple, Google, digital health startups (e.g., 23andMe)
Smart city	IBM, Verizon, Samsung, Google
New retail and omnichannel shopping	Major brand leaders, retail stores and digital startups, Amazon, Alibaba, Walmart, Target

2. Enhance product ontology

In consumer settings, Netflix comprehends the ontology of movies across various genres, languages, moods, etc. as experienced by its subscribers and uses that knowledge to make superior recommendations.[8] Airbnb tracks not just the room each individual rented but also other dimensions such as the places of interest they visited, where they dined, and the shows they watched. The company's ability to expand the scope of its datagraph allows it to develop targeted, personalized recommendations.[9] Similarly, industrials must expand their datagraphs' ontologies to deliver superior customer value.

Look at Mineral, the company within Alphabet's corporate structure that's focused on agriculture. The datafication of agriculture is piecemeal, but the potential benefits are significant. Mineral operates under a general belief that, as its website asserts, "most companies are not collecting the quantity, diversity or quality of data needed to take full advantage of machine learning. That's why we built tools to better capture, curate, clean, and augment multimodal data; and assembled our own bootstrap ag dataset." And since there's no single mode of data collection suited to every agriculture task or crop, the company "began with a plant rover that could capture huge quantities of high quality images, and over time expanded to building generalized perception technology that can work across platforms such as robots, third party farm equipment, drones, sentinel devices and mobile phones." Mineral can develop detailed crop graphs and speed up the digitization of agriculture thanks to the increasing use of multidimensional datasets in new technologies and approaches. Over time, such insights will help a broad set of companies in the farming and food industries to develop an end-to-end understanding with real-time data from farm to fork to reduce inefficiency and enhance sustainable agriculture.

Suppose an automobile manufacturer wants to move from selling cars to providing transportation services. In that case, it must expand its datagraph's ontology to include new and diverse data elements: locations and destinations of travel across days and months; preferred modes of travel for different purposes, such as leisure versus business; price sensitivity for different trips; and so on. In doing so, it competes against mobility companies like Uber, Didi, and Lyft, which are focused on understanding how individuals use different modes of transportation 24-7-365. To achieve the goal of proactively offering transport solutions that cater to individual needs and preferences at an acceptable cost, these companies must gather accurate and specific data. This data will help them create a comprehensive ontology of personal transport needs and priorities.[10]

Industrial leaders must invest in developing their ontologies to understand datagraphs as the new differentiation driver. Companies that fail to do so, and treat data as merely an operational tactic, miss out on the network effects their digital twins could capture. To develop richer ontologies, the industrials must pay attention to the veracity of data fed into datagraphs. At Honeywell, it is crucial to determine whether the failure of machines and systems in client locations is caused by factors within its control or by the actions of its customers and partners. This also applies to automakers like GM and Ford, which rely on complex supply chains. Digital twins with end-to-end monitoring must encompass supply chains, including dataflows and ontologies, to ensure accuracy. Misclassification can lead to wasted efforts to address problems, especially when multiple entities are involved.

Industrial ontology relies on language that explains data structures in various situations to understand how machines work and how they affect customer productivity. This is important as devices move from electromechanical to digital-industrial architectures, encompassing hardware, software, data, and connectivity protocols. Improving and expanding the vocabulary of machine operations (and failures) helps companies use datagraphs to create efficient machines and improve customer outcomes. And this becomes a necessary precondition to take advantage of Gen AI.

An understanding of how concepts are interconnected in industrial datagraphs has yet to develop fully. Companies tend to store data in separate departments with unique database structures, which makes it challenging to create graphical representations of ontology. However, major industrial companies like Siemens, Bosch, Rolls-Royce, Honeywell, and ABB have developed graphs to depict the interrelated knowledge of their machines and operations.[11] Cloud computing providers like Amazon Web Services, Microsoft Azure, and IBM offer tools and applications to aid this process.

Capturing industrial product-in-use data will require fitting devices and drawing up new protocols on machines in the short run and, in the long run, infusing communication capabilities into products. Telemetry has become more potent, enabling automatic data transmission from remote settings over radio frequencies, infrared, ultrasonic, Bluetooth devices, Wi-Fi, satellite, and cable.

Large language models (LLMs) represent a significant advancement in the digital realm, promising to transform industrial domains through learned knowledge. So far these models have impacted asset-light sectors (search, customer interactions, education) with early applications focused on summarizing articles, drafting stories, creating images, and engaging in long conversations. Those uses are relevant and applicable in industrial settings but are not strategic. What's strategic—and a potential game-changer—is when an LLM can be trained to understand the reasons for machine failures, uncover previously hidden relationships between concepts, identify the underlying root causes more easily, recommend what to do in response, and determine how best to redesign the next machine. What excites us is that industrial machines will develop "eyes and ears" and be able to transmit more-comprehensive data with sounds, images, and moving images that explain how machines operate in the field in multimodal forms. This will allow industrials to use Gen AI to figure out relevant and targeted ways to unlock more value for customers.[12]

We agree with Elliott Grant, CEO of Mineral, that machine learning is well suited to agriculture in areas such as using a satellite image to count leaves or pixels of wheat or to classify weeds. Here, what matters is not absolute accuracy. If a machine can classify 90 percent of the weeds among the millions of plants in a field in milliseconds, it is preferable to humans taking hours to walk the field. In many industrial settings, machines can confer accuracy at scale at affordable price points.[13]

Industrial data can be complex, and machine learning and Gen AI can offer valuable solutions. As model sizes proliferate each year and experiments with models in health care, software, security, and logistics become more common, it's essential to consider using LLMs to improve the understanding of industrial ontologies. Companies that embrace LLMs will likely have an advantage over those that don't.

3. Conquer with AI at customer moments that matter

Industrial datagraphs and updated knowledge ontology can be power-ful tools, but they require complementary algorithms to provide personalized insights for specific customers to achieve superior results. The algorithms help carry out four interrelated types of analyses.

Descriptive analysis allows an industrial company to understand what happened based on an interdependent set of datagraphs instead of independent systems of records. While dashboards provide static statistics such as reliability, mean time to failure, significant sources of defects, and other indices of machine performance, datagraphs allow executives to delve deeper. They can analyze the patterns of machine performance across different settings by linking information across domains and companies. And datagraphs can increasingly be queried through conversations, making it easy for business executives to take timely actions instead of relying on data experts to conduct analyses.

Diagnostic analysis enables a company to understand why some-thing happened by carrying out root-cause analyses of machine failures and mapping them to controllable and uncontrollable factors. Instead of treating each industrial machine as independent, data-graphs allow for a more profound examination of the reasons for fail-ure or deviations from expected levels. Did the use of a component from a specific supplier cause underperformance? Did the customer deviate from the suggested operating procedures? Having an inte-grated ontology of critical concepts and interrelationships in a graph structure helps make this level of diagnostic analysis possible. With well-trained Gen AI, the diagnostic analysis would be faster and more accurate, too.

Predictive analysis tackles the question of what could happen using graph structures. Knowing how machines work in tandem with other devices and equipment in diverse locations, executives can forecast likely failures or performance degradation; predictions based on in-terdependent graph structures are more effective than those of siloed models. Executives can then develop rules to tackle them, explore alternatives through simulations, and assign responsibilities in advance.

Prescriptive analysis asks: How should we help our customers get the best from our machines and equipment? What could we do to rectify problems immediately with, for instance, over-the-air software updates or easy-to-follow instructions? This kind of analysis helps companies develop an end-to-end view of how products operate in the field across different permutations and combinations to assess the sequence of steps to tackle customer problems. The industrials can develop models that place prescriptive analytics at the center of delivering efficient, differentiated, personalized value to customers.

These four analyses, inherent to the data value chain, must be coordinated to connect data to business results, as figure 3-2 illustrates. It's not about studying data to gain insights at an abstract level; it's about linking data to business results, as we see in born-digital companies such as Netflix, Spotify, Uber, and Tesla.

The data value chain is more than just a onetime solution for emergencies or exceptions. It's a crucial part of Gen AI, which combines large language models with gigabytes of data represented by hundreds of millions of text tokens. This chain is as important as the value chain that turns raw materials into finished products for industrial manufacturers.

FIGURE 3-2

Data value chain and four types of analysis

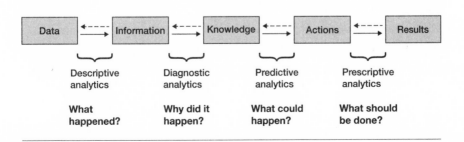

As we move forward, understanding the complementary data value chain will be essential for offering customers precisely what they require at the appropriate moment. Gen AI is a crucial tool that links data to business value and transforms unexplored business potential into genuine value for industries and their clients. This means that AI is not just a technical matter but something senior managers must take seriously.

Rolls-Royce utilizes the four types of analysis to benefit in two ways. First, while each airline has data on only its own aircrafts, Rolls-Royce has the vantage point to analyze product-in-use data across all its customers, which it must do with the highest security, privacy, and confidentiality levels. This broad scope of access to data allows the company to develop superior insights to solve customer problems. Second, by analyzing rich and dynamic datagraphs using AI, Rolls-Royce can design and develop products of even higher quality. The result is that more customers will want to purchase its products instead of those from competitors—which do not have such feedback effects—increasing the scale, scope, and speed of its datagraphs.

Facing New Battles

Product-in-use data is fast becoming a game-changer for industrial competition. Previously, such data was difficult to obtain, but with the help of tripartite twins, it is now easier to track and trace. These twins provide real-time data for each company to create its unique datagraph, which is proprietary and grows in value due to data network effects.

Through analyzing how products are used, companies can develop personalized solutions for customers and better understand their products' operations and interactions. Utilizing industrial datagraphs, this approach is becoming the next frontier of competition. As companies continue to gather information about their products and how they add value for customers, they can gain sharper insights

and make better recommendations, giving them an edge ⟨
petitors that have yet to embrace industrial datagraphs.

By now you likely have a good understanding of fusion in ⟨
strategy (discussed in chapter 1), how real-time data can be
uncover winning strategies in asset-light, direct-to-consum⟨
tors (chapter 2), and how algorithms can combine with indu
datagraphs to lead to major competitive shifts in asset-heavy se
(this chapter). The digital world is expanding rapidly, and indus
businesses must think strategically about how to navigate it. W
are the opportunities to create and capture value, and how sho
we prepare for the challenges ahead? In the next chapter, we w
delve deeper into how datagraphs can assist industrial companies
achieving victory in various competitive battles.

CHAPTER 4

Four Battlegrounds

C OMPANIES LABEL MANY PRODUCTS, SUCH AS SPEAKERS, doorbells, and coffee machines, "smart" nowadays merely because they have relatively more digital features than their analog counterparts do. However, digital displays, software functionality, and network connectivity do *not* make a product smart.

A similar pattern emerges from the announcements made by the industrials. Their focus is squarely on connectivity and automation: the autonomy of vehicles such as cars, trucks, tractors, and haulers; software applications to fine-tune machines and connect them with related equipment; Bluetooth and cellular networks; and digital dashboards that display a wide array of metrics. Industrial machinery that is called smart isn't really that smart either.

The industrials need to change their perceptions. To be truly smart, industrial products should be able to capture and track real-time, product-in-use data and take advantage of data network effects. By utilizing insights from datagraphs and algorithms, product designs will continually evolve and deliver more value for customers. This chapter focuses on the battlegrounds that emerge when industrial products become digital.

Fusion Strategy Builds on Industrial Datagraphs and AI

For over forty years, executives have been appropriately taught that in order to succeed, they have to choose one of three generic strategies—cost leadership, differentiation, or focus—that best matches their industry's structure.[1] But those strategies don't deliver optimal results in today's era of datagraphs and AI.

Traditional strategy's roots lie in another era, when companies analyzed data from products as sold. That has led many CEOs to mistakenly assume that the impact of digital technologies will be minimal. They treat digital technologies as tools to preserve cost leadership, provide features such as connectivity, or help maintain focus.

But as the experience of the asset-light industries shows, to thrive and even survive, the industrials will have to capture data in real time and develop datagraphs based on product-in-use information to transform their businesses. Doing so will redraw the competitive landscape, creating intersecting businesses that will force incumbents to compete with the digitals. In addition to the horizontal and vertical integration of sectors, diagonal links will emerge across unrelated sectors, redistributing value among different groups of players.

Companies must think through their strategies against the backdrop of the shifts in the competitive landscape that digital technologies will cause. That's where industrial datagraphs will help CEOs explore strategy options and map new directions. They must ask two questions (see figure 4-1):

One, what is the *reach* of our industrial datagraphs? Do they stop with the design of digital twins to deliver efficiency? Or do they extend into customers' operations to optimize their outcomes? This dimension shows the scale of the datagraph.

Two, how *rich* is our industrial datagraph? Is it based on a limited number of dimensions? Or is it multidimensional, capable of capturing the interdependencies between all the machinery, equipment, and subsystems our customers use to realize their business goals? Is it

FIGURE 4-1

Fusion strategies in the different battlegrounds

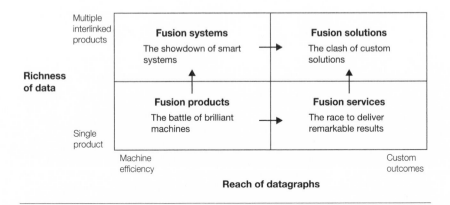

multimodal and capable of collecting numbers, text, images, sounds, and videos? This reflects the scope of a datagraph, which can extend from a single machine to several machines made by the same company, to a portfolio of machines from different companies.

The answers to these questions surface four fusion battlegrounds with specific winning strategies: fusion products, fusion services, fusion systems, and fusion solutions.

The industrials will have to make choices and pursue one of the four battlegrounds even as they explore the others. Most will start by pursuing strategies for fusion products. Then they have to evaluate the opportunities and challenges of enhancing customers' business outcomes by providing fusion services or pursuing ways to turn products and services into fusion systems so that they operate more efficiently and effectively. The final prize is fusion solutions.

This exercise will allow the industrials to understand how they can create and capture value, evaluate how rivals' strategies threaten them, and determine the resource reallocations they must make to defend or develop another strategy. Thus, the fusion strategies framework is inherently dynamic—not static. Let's discuss each battleground in turn.

Commit to Fusion Products

Fusion products are designed with telemetry to observe their performance in real time. The key is collecting product-in-use data, so companies can analyze it and find ways to improve performance systematically. Aggregated across their installed bases, the industrials can create data network effects and continually enhance machine efficiency (shown in the bottom-left quadrant in figure 4-1).

Fusion products will contain purpose-built chips for AI and machine learning, which companies can use to monitor products' performance in the field. Tripartite digital twins will support design and delivery so that the industrial can analyze, develop, and implement rules to make the machines perform at higher levels and minimize downtime through predictive maintenance. The company can capture value by offering maintenance and productivity programs as services for a price or by providing them for free to ensure customer loyalty.

The investment thesis to justify digitalizing industrial machines—incorporating telematics functionality, adopting modular computer architectures, and infusing data analytics—may not be straightforward. So, many industrials may be tempted to double down on designing better industrial products and pushing the quality frontier to make the product the best in its class instead of investing in the unfamiliar digital domain. That's rational but myopic.

Sure, the sensors, intelligent cameras, GPS instruments, ambient condition probes, and performance monitoring modules will seem expensive on a stand-alone basis. However, the industrials' focus shouldn't be on what a single sensor can do but on how a suite of sensors can collectively provide real-time, product-in-use data to the operations center. They should be thinking about how fusion products generate and use data network effects; the reasoning should be based on the insights gleaned from knowing how well the machines perform under different conditions in the field. And the analysis should be about using insights to win in the market.

All of this calls for progressively adding digital capabilities to industrial designs until the product reaches a fused state technologically, physically, and commercially. The objective should be to design products that can be tracked continuously, updated from the cloud, and controlled remotely, which will require programmable hardware and embedded software. Taking these steps will help the industrials develop product datagraphs from the beginning of their digital efforts, rather than as an afterthought. That's what the automotive industry has learned from Tesla; the agriculture and construction sectors from John Deere and CNH Industrial; and the building and construction sectors from Honeywell and Siemens.

You may be familiar with *power by the hour*, a long-standing practice in aviation. The idea is to offer a complete engine and accessory replacement service on a fixed-cost-per-flying-hour basis. Customers found it compelling as they paid only for engines that performed to the standard with 100 percent uptime; accessing machine capacity by paying per use is commonplace now.

Rolls-Royce pioneered the idea in 1962, using the few (relatively primitive) sensors on aircraft to track on-wing performance. Today Rolls-Royce uses engine performance data to remove the risk related to unscheduled maintenance events and make maintenance costs planned and predictable. Its sixty-year-old trademarked phrase, "power by the hour," is commonly understood in the industry, as other manufacturers of aircraft engines—such as GE and Pratt & Whitney—followed its approach.

Fusion products aren't only those that move, such as automobiles, tractors, and aircraft; they can also be stationary, such as buildings, glass windows, and gas turbines. Any industrial product can be reimagined as a fusion product by adding sensors, programmable hardware, software, and cloud connectivity. That will require the end-to-end rethinking of product architectures, making them resemble programmable machines whose software can be continually updated over the air.

Every industrial company should focus on this kind of thinking by learning from adjacent arenas. Unlike the asset-light sectors, the digitalization of industrial products will take time, so companies should start immediately. Doing so will enable the pioneers to gain first- and fast-mover advantages.

Surround Fusion Products with Fusion Services

The transformation from industrial to fusion products is the foundation, a necessary step. Only after that do alternative trajectories become available. One to consider is the shift from products to services.

Industrials could offer services by extending the reach of their datagraphs into customers' operations. (This is along the horizontal axis of figure 4-1, as the lower-right quadrant shows.) Strategy here isn't about revamping the customer service function with AI-driven chatbots, restructuring arrangements with dealers for a larger share of service revenues, or forming risk-return sharing with third-party service providers. It's about making fusion products work deeper inside customer operations to improve business outcomes. The strategy's success must be measured not only by additional revenues or profits but also by the significance of the industrials' roles in boosting customer performance.

The industrials must rely on tripartite digital twins to pursue a fusion services strategy. Instead of limiting them to tracking product performance, companies must extend them by interlinking the product with the service performance twins. While the former can be deployed by the industrial, a fusion services strategy will require the permission of, and cooperation with, customers and, in some cases, partners. The industrial must earn the right to gather granular data to understand how it can enhance customers' performances by improving its machines.

Creating data hooks to tap into a broader data stream expands the scope of service datagraphs. Think how knowledgeable an aircraft engine manufacturer would be if it amassed data—at scale and speed—across all the engines deployed worldwide in near real time. The data would create service datagraphs and serve as the basis of a shift from products to services.

To embark on a fusion services strategy, Rolls-Royce set up R^2 Data Labs in 2018. It has been steadily working since then to gain an edge with data; the Labs help Rolls-Royce understand how to use data to generate efficiencies, reduce emissions, pinpoint cost savings, and identify new revenue opportunities. Rolls-Royce's services have been focused on engine health monitoring data, building on its long-standing competencies in using AI. It delivers services by relying on experienced data analysts who understand what anomalies might mean and make operational recommendations.

For example, Rolls-Royce analyzes fuel consumption patterns based on product-in-use data such as the routes aircraft take, the altitudes at which they fly, the weather conditions during flight, the speed at which they fly, and the load the aircraft is carrying. The company receives more than seventy trillion data points each year from its engines.[2] By leveraging the power of datagraphs, Rolls-Royce helps customers be at the frontier of fuel efficiency; improving an engine's fuel efficiency by 1 percent results in approximately $30 billion in savings in the global aviation sector over the next 15 years.[3]

In another instance, an engine's parameters might be out of range due to a change in conditions or a recording error. While the system would detect and record such fluctuations as a problem, it is up to human experts to determine whether it's a serious issue or a false alert. Historically, human skill and expertise was the only way to decipher what happened. But given the power of large language models, robust AI systems working with humans can make fusion services effective, monetizable, and profitable.

Thanks to the insights it gains from advanced analytics, Rolls-Royce is in a strong position to enter into savings-based contracts, and to ask airlines to share with it a portion of the unlocked value from guaranteed savings. Could Rolls-Royce succeed with fusion services?

Yes, it could. Will it? It has an edge. Given its digital and data foundations, it has a first-mover advantage over rivals such as GE and Pratt & Whitney. It also needs to assess if it should explore this opportunity independently or partner with others from a position of strength.

Wrapping services around products is a multithreaded journey with flywheel effects. It starts with the industrials designing ways to seamlessly interconnect their product performance twins with service performance twins at customer locations. That creates data network effects that aren't limited to product performance but extend to service delivery. It subsequently enables the industrial company to better understand how its products drive customer productivity and performance. The data from the performance twins, aggregated across different settings, will show areas where proactive interventions can take place and how the industrial can fine-tune products so that their value to the customer rises. As more customers accept the service propositions, industrials can invest in digital functionality to interlink the tripartite digital twins.

Skeptical executives may wonder if customers will grant them access to their operations. They will, but only if the fusion services' prescriptions prove valuable. Of course, the industrial company must earn the right to penetrate customer operations by guaranteeing the privacy of data and analyzing customer data anonymously. Customers will allow the industrials to connect their machines with embedded data hooks in their operations if they believe that the resulting services are better than those offered by third-party providers that are unlikely to benefit from data network effects. Even services that customers develop will have limitations because the heuristics can be derived only from their operations.

Integrate Products into Fusion Systems

Let's look at another trajectory. The digitalization of industrial machines offers new ways to create efficiency, not just by improving each product with its tripartite twin but also by optimizing a higher-order system of interconnected products. The shift from products to systems occurs on the vertical axis of figure 4-1, which depicts the richness of datagraphs (the upper-left quadrant).

When you visit a large farm, construction site, oil refinery, mine, or factory, you will see machines and equipment made by several industrial companies. Complex systems comprising multiple digital industrial products and subsystems are the norm for the industrials' customers. Once the system integrator has linked different machines, companies manage the operations or rely on third-party operators.

An industrial seeking to be a fusion systems integrator should construct datagraphs first by digitally connecting all its machines and then progressively expanding them to interlink with those of partners (and competitors) with application programming interfaces (APIs). It should start with structured data and then expand to unstructured multimedia data that can be fed into AI and ML applications. The objective is to construct a system-level datagraph with the same underlying knowledge ontology that Google, LinkedIn, and Amazon use, linking related concepts and entities.

A fusion systems integrator is proficient in assembling systems but doesn't stop there. Its differentiation comes from the data it ingests across each system's tripartite twins in operation and the resulting data network effects. It develops insights into why fusion systems underperform in the field relative to the designed levels by analyzing data from different conditions.

Customers find this strategy valuable because no industrial machine is an island; efficiency isn't the level of reliability or uptime of a single machine, but that of a system of machines that operate together. When one product fails, the entire system fails. The reliability and uptime of individual machines are less valuable because the weakest part of the system creates the problem. However, the fusion systems integrator can minimize systemic disruptions by expanding the scope of datagraphs beyond its products and tracking, analyzing, and predicting system failures better than its customers. It can monetize this knowledge by charging systems integration fees, annual fees to connect additional machines, and by selling software updates that ensure the fusion systems operate as specified.

Systems integrators in the industrial age gained competencies in managing large complex projects by deploying and redeploying human talent with expertise in engineering (think Schlumberger and Halliburton) or IT systems (think Infosys, Accenture, Tata Consultancy Services, and Deloitte). However, would-be fusion systems leaders, such as Siemens, Honeywell, and Rockwell Automation, will succeed if they develop competencies in gathering product-in-use data with less emphasis on human talent and more on combining intelligent humans and powerful machines.

The aircraft industry is showing the way. In 2020 Rolls-Royce established Yocova (You + Collaboration = Value) as an experimental path to digital transformation, with Singapore Airlines as its first major industry partner.[4] Yocova aims to offer an open, end-to-end system for the aviation industry to connect, collaborate, control their data, and buy and sell digital solutions through a global marketplace. This organization came about because Rolls-Royce recognized that industries that once worked in silos could thrive if they were organized as collaborative networks powered by data. As such system-level integration gains traction with more enterprises joining, the full value will be unlocked.

Airlines exchange data across reservation systems with code sharing (Sabre), route optimization, and frequent flyer points (Oneworld, Star Alliance). Seamless coordination is essential for safety across many different entities. Yet this sector hasn't attained the full potential of fusion systems, with data stuck in siloed databases in areas such as operations, marketing, and maintenance. Given the amount of data being moved between engines, aircraft, engine health monitoring departments, and operators, opportunities will emerge to create system-level datagraphs and experiments with AI and machine learning.

Expect more industries to occupy the upper-left quadrant of figure 4-1 because of the industrial use of data and AI. Even if an industrial doesn't plan to pursue a fusion systems strategy, it should understand the power of the system tripartite twin—the three twins taken together—and how datagraphs unlock value. Doing so will help it figure out how its fusion products should work with one or more systems so that rival offerings can't substitute for its products.

Solve Customer Problems, One at a Time, for Many

The final fusion strategy combines products, services, and systems to solve each customer's unique problems. It requires an outside-in perspective and can be done only by developing a rich set of datagraphs and reaching deeper into customers' operations.

Industrials must become extensions of their customers' operations by designing solution performance twins, a specific type of performance twin, and becoming experts at solving customer problems in ways that no other company, or even the customer, can. Thus, the power of a fusion solutions strategy stems from solving customer problems at speed and adapting solutions as conditions change.

To pursue a fusion solutions strategy, industrials must start by earning their customers' trust to understand their needs at a granular level. Doing so will enable them to architect solutions with an integrated suite of products, services, and systems that affect the customers' performance.

Then, the industrial companies must access data at the level of detail they need to construct proprietary datagraphs and leverage data network effects across settings. Armed with these datagraphs, a fusion solutions strategy calls for developing algorithms that deliver customized solutions to every customer. The industrials can monetize solutions through outcome-based contracts and profit-sharing agreements.

The fusion solutions provider must be seen to be unbiased in that it doesn't use only its products. It must knit together the best possible solutions to solve customer problems in a spirit of partnership with rivals. Solutions combine systems and services, but they aren't one-offs; they can be refined continuously based on the industrial's knowledge and experience. Unlike the other industrial datagraphs, which start with the manufacturer's machines, the solutions datagraph begins with the customer's problems (the top-right quadrant of figure 4-1).

Consider the example of a new airline, Riyadh Air, set up by Saudi Arabia to remake the country as a tourist destination and compete against the successful airlines in the region, such as Emirates, Etihad Airways, and Qatar Airways. Riyadh Air will be looking for partners that can draw on their expertise and experience in aviation to provide solutions.

Could Rolls-Royce step into the solutions space with its expertise in designing intelligent engines and become a pivotal partner? It has an edge because of what it has already set up, with Singapore Airlines as a partner (the Yocova initiative discussed earlier). Since it has mastered digital platform integration, it could outline the benefits of Yocova for Riyadh Air, showing how Rolls-Royce can push the frontier of predictive maintenance, fuel efficiency optimization, and fleet management.

Its advanced engine design capabilities, with digital twin technology, can expand the scope of its tripartite twins. So, Rolls-Royce could work with Airbus and Boeing to refine aircraft designs. The knowledge ontology that Rolls-Royce has accumulated could reveal specific ways the new airline can unlock opportunities not available to others. Rolls-Royce must be prepared to orchestrate relationships with a portfolio of partners to be a credible fusion solutions company capable of defining the next generation of air travel.

Such a large opportunity is rare in industrial settings, and it will be instructive to watch how existing and new players fight for the opportunity.

A fusion solutions strategy will focus on understanding customer problems in microscopic detail and assembling the best products, services, and systems to solve them. Fusion solutions providers must be perceived to be trusted solutions architects and tie their profits to customer success. To win with fusion solutions, the industrials must shift from the well-known maxim Made by Us to the new logic of Solved by Us.

The New Strategy Battlegrounds

Four battlegrounds for value creation and capture have emerged as the industrial world digitalizes. The fusion strategy framework is dynamic; a company should not choose and defend a single strategy. Rather, the company should start with a fusion products strategy and then migrate to one of the other three strategies.

Each of the four battlegrounds has a distinct focus on where the industrials can unlock value. The first is the battle for brilliant machines, or the fusion products strategy, where the value is predominantly created by digitalizing industrial products and delivering them at the highest performance levels (the lower-left quadrant of figure 4-1). The industrials must compete against traditional competitors that may be digitalizing their machines at different scales, scopes, or speeds, as well as newer companies that can design machines afresh and develop new competencies with data and AI.

Then there's the second battleground (the lower-right quadrant of figure 4-1), which we term the race for remarkable results, or the fusion services strategy. This strategy relates to industrial machines embedded deep in customer operations to help unlock more ways to improve the customer's financial performance. The race puts the industrials in competition with traditional players and third-party service providers that are closer to customer operations, as well as customers that take the responsibility to optimize machines to deliver their business goals.

The third battleground is the upper-left quadrant, labeled the showdown of smart systems, or the fusion systems strategy. In this segment, interlinked systems compete against independent products to unlock value. And those industrial companies with fusion products indirectly compete and cooperate with them.

Finally, the fourth battleground is the clash of custom solutions, or the fusion solutions strategy (the top-right quadrant). The competition in this segment is between companies and ecosystems jockeying to deliver solutions for customers while believing they can do what's best without any external help.

To win battles, invite and involve partners

The strategy we teach in classrooms today is firm-centric in focus. By contrast, the fusion strategy framework proposes that companies balance owning assets with developing relationships to access complementary resources. Every company can be part of multiple ecosystems, with the scale, scope, and speed of datagraphs defining where, when, and how they should partner in different ecosystems.

Fusion strategies are network-centric and intersect the business and data domains in overlapping ecosystems. The value proposition of a fusion products strategy is based not on what happens inside the industrial company but on how its products perform in the field, with the power of the performance twin unlocking new value. When industrials go beyond the fusion products strategy, they go deeper into customers' and partners' operations (the horizontal and vertical axes, respectively) with interconnected dataflows and interlinked systems architectures. They must co-opt and cocreate value with customers and partners, so it will be critical for them to navigate emerging ecosystems and define the key data elements.

Datagraphs that support systems integration strategies will invariably involve data from rivals. To assure competitors that their data will be used effectively, the industrials may need to design operating models with clear rules of engagement. Just as Amazon Web Services must ensure that its data security protocols satisfy Netflix as a customer, especially since Prime Video is a rival, fusion strategies need a culture that treasures privacy, security, and data integrity.

Don't be stuck in the same battleground

An oft-leveled criticism is that strategy frameworks are usually static. However, the fusion strategy framework is inherently dynamic. It depicts choices that industrials can make at a given point in time while exploring pathways to the future.

Fusion products create value by improving uptime on the company's machines. Fusion services do it by bundling services with fusion products to enhance customer productivity. Fusion systems add value by ensuring uptime on all the equipment used by the customer, not just the industrial's own products. And fusion solutions are designed to solve customer problems in their entirety. Thus, each fusion strategy creates *additional* pools of value, so an industrial should develop a road map to develop and deploy all four strategies.

. . .

Venture capitalist Marc Andreessen declared in 2011 that "software is eating the world."[5] He was right: digital technologies have fueled innovation, disruption, and transformation in many consumer businesses. These technologies are now driving dramatic changes in industrial companies too.

Meanwhile, the developed world has forsaken its competencies in creating value in asset-heavy sectors such as manufacturing, transportation, farming, health care, and logistics, enamored with the value that can be made in asset-light sectors. In 2020 Andreessen stated, "It's time to build"—not in the ways of the industrial age but in new ways that fuse the physical and the digital.[6]

It's time for the industrials to build the fusion future. Traditionally they've won because of the advantages rooted in tangible assets, such as scale, design, patents, quality, and customer satisfaction. Those will remain relevant, but fusion strategies add a new dimension when digital technologies transform industrial companies. The industrials will enjoy mastery over data network effects with their algorithms refining products, processes, and modes of service delivery.

Fusion strategy will drive the transformation of industrial companies. Any incremental adjustments to the strategies perfected during the waning decades of the industrial era will prove ineffective. Machines will be digitalized, processes will be streamlined, and service delivery will be enhanced with software, data, and analytics. The approaches that work will need to be strategic rather than tactical or technical.

The industrial winners will embrace digital technologies to forge the future. They would be wise to recognize the power of industrial datagraphs to defend their current businesses. And, importantly, they must use datagraphs to lay out pathways to develop new business models suited to win tomorrow's competitive battles, as we will explore in the second part of the book.

PART TWO

VECTORS
OF VALUE

CHAPTER 5

The Battle of Brilliant Machines

ON AUGUST 2, 2006—MONTHS BEFORE STEVE JOBS unveiled the iPhone—Elon Musk made an announcement: "The overarching purpose of Tesla Motors (and the reason I am funding the company) is to help expedite the move from a mine-and-burn hydrocarbon economy towards a solar electric economy."

The auto industry barely took notice of what Musk called his master plan. Ten years later, on July 20, 2016, "master plan, part deux" promised a full line of products with a self-driving capability that, through fleet learning, would be ten times safer than manual driving. The reactions were mostly skeptical, from "cash flow sinkhole" to "overly ambitious" to "no different than what the incumbents have announced."

By the time Musk announced "master plan part 3" on April 5, 2023, focused on "a sustainable energy civilization," the analysts were divided into two camps.[1] One was disappointed by the lack of a new vehicle road map, and the other was excited by the underpinnings of the vehicle platform and the inner workings of the role for automobiles to lead toward sustainable energy—the original vision announced in 2006.

Future business historians will record how much Tesla shaped the transformation of the auto sector and its contribution to sustainable energy. For now, the company is very much part of the zeitgeist of the business world. It wasn't even on the radar of the auto industry incumbents in 2006; in 2016 it was, at best, in their peripheral vision. By the early 2020s Tesla was squarely at the center of the automotive industry, as it spurred transformation of not just the energy source that powers the product but the very concept of what an automobile is and will be in the future.

On August 30, 2021, Tesla announced that it had designed a large semiconductor chip, which it calls the D-1, to run the machine-learning algorithms that control its Autopilot self-driving system and Dojo, its neural-network-training supercomputer. By July 2023 it had bought as many GPU units from Nvidia as the chip company could deliver while investing around $1 billion to supercharge its Dojo initiative. A decade ago, no one would have expected that an automobile manufacturer would want to design one of the fastest supercomputers in the world.

While the Austin-headquartered company has previously developed smaller chips that interpret the inputs from the sensors and cameras in its vehicles, creating the D-1 chip and the Dojo supercomputer was more challenging and expensive. The effort is central to Tesla's future, since the company needs the D-1 to improve Autopilot. The self-driving system no longer uses radar or laser imaging, detection, and ranging (LiDAR) to paint objects and surfaces with lasers so that automobiles can "see" the world around them in three dimensions. Instead, it relies on computer vision to make sense of the visual information gathered by the vehicles' cameras. The new approach involves training the computer to recognize and interpret the visual world to achieve autonomous driving capabilities.

Specifically, Tesla uses a neural network known as a transformer, which receives inputs from the eight cameras in each vehicle to understand its operating conditions. Using a camera-only system is computationally more demanding; the Tesla Vision algorithm must reconstruct a real-time map of each vehicle's surroundings from camera feeds rather than from sensors that capture pictures directly.

Tesla enjoys an advantage over rivals because it gathers more data than other automobile manufacturers. Each of the more than four million Tesla cars on the road sends back video feeds from eight cameras, and over one thousand employees label those images to help train the network. Just as Ford vertically integrated in the early 1900s, even mining coal and iron ore and manufacturing glass for its automobiles, Tesla's designing the D-1 chip symbolizes the company's evolution into a latter-day integrated automobile manufacturer that makes everything for its fusion products itself, from electric batteries, silicon chips, and software to a charging network and service centers.

Its fusion products epitomize a potent dual threat to the incumbents in the automobile industry. Tesla makes powerful, environment-friendly, and sleek vehicles. The company has also invested in developing advanced technologies for digital connectivity and data collection. Each car's cameras and twelve ultrasonic sensors collect data in real time, and the company's machine-learning algorithms constantly analyze the data to improve its operating system (OS).

Just as Apple develops and deploys new OS for the iPhone, Tesla periodically updates its vehicles' OS. Because of over-the-air software updates, Tesla owners wake up to a new automobile nearly every morning. For instance, in November 2019 a Tesla aficionado, Brandon Bernicky, tweeted at Elon Musk: "Thoughts on saving dashcam footage when honking the horn?"[2] "Yeah, makes sense," replied Musk hours later. On December 24 the feature rolled out over the air, enabling Tesla drivers to record a snippet from the front video camera when they honk and store it on a USB drive. An update cycle of six weeks, rather than months or years, is unprecedented in the automobile industry.

Moreover, all Tesla's vehicles operate on the same network, so every driver helps the entire network of cars improve—what the company terms *fleet learning.* It designed the Model S to be a sophisticated computer on wheels, Musk has often said, pointing out that Tesla is a software company as much as it is a hardware company. We see it as a data and AI company that makes physical machines—in our parlance, fusion products.

Tesla has created a performance twin of every car it has made, not just a digital twin of every model as it was designed or a twin of the assembly line that created it. The sensors in each car provide data in real time about how the vehicle is performing on the road; the company's AI/ML systems study the data in real time; and Tesla uses the most relevant data-driven insights to continuously improve all its cars' autonomous driving systems. Moreover, the AI interprets the data and determines whether a vehicle works as intended or needs maintenance. With many issues, Tesla's digital experts ensure that problems can be fixed with software updates; for instance, they can adjust the regenerative braking levels to reduce collision risks and adjust door rattling via over-the-air software updates. On average, it issues a major software update once every month.

The company's tripartite twins help it optimize future products with generative design, the emerging technology that applies AI to optimize designs. By aggregating real-time data from thousands of products in the field, the digital twins simulate the performance and conditions faced by the fusion product over its lifetime. Armed with this data, generative design software tweaks Tesla's product designs and simulates performance in real-world situations until it arrives at a solution that satisfies the company's goals.

Although Tesla went through manufacturing hell to kick-start its production lines in the historic NUMMI plant in Fremont, California, which Toyota and GM had operated until 2010, it has transformed the automobile manufacturing process with digital technologies. It uses a highly vertically integrated and automated manufacturing process involving over 160 robots—including 10 of the world's largest, each named after one of Marvel's X-Men. Tesla's AI-based systems allow for the autonomous and continuous improvement of its manufacturing process. When vehicles on the road experience even minor problems, such as a constant vibration in the windows, the data is communicated to Tesla's robots on the line, which refine the window installation process.

Tesla delivered 1.31 million vehicles in 2022 and is expected to deliver about 1.8 million in 2023. By August 2023 its market capitalization hovered around $900 billion, placing it among the top ten most valuable companies; its market cap is larger than those of the next nine most valuable carmakers put together. Thus, Tesla, the least valuable automobile manufacturer in 2000, enters its third decade as the world's most valuable—and intriguing—automaker thanks to its fusion products.

The Product Paradigm Shifts

To us fusion strategists, designing and delivering cars with more computing power isn't enough to make them brilliant machines. That's because the intelligence in today's cars tends to be limited to how the cars were designed, manufactured, and delivered to consumers. The companies that produce the latest models of these vehicles have scant data on how their products are driven. Their views of data's role in their product strategies are stuck in the world of systems of record (often referred to as data at rest), unable to compete against companies that have started to leverage real-time data in use (often referred to as data in motion).

What, beyond digital bells and whistles, would make automobiles the archetype of a fusion product? When cars are infused with machine learning to continually improve how they steer in actual driving conditions, and when driving rules are continuously refined and enhanced with insights from datagraphs and algorithms. That's what Waymo—a subsidiary of Alphabet, not a traditional automaker—is aiming for. It may not be involved in manufacturing, but Waymo wants to design the brain that powers future automobiles. In that vision, the strategic thinking is that the physical product—metal, plastic, and tires—may not be the differentiator, but the intelligence that drives the car will be. Waymo's vision of the most experienced driving system is a digital artifact that learns continually.

What makes Waymo's AI-driven system the most experienced, you ask? It's not how its brain is programmed with general driving rules and navigation routines when the automobile is designed and built, but how it dynamically learns from the collective experience of a fleet of cars on the road.[3] Waymo's integrated suite of LiDAR and radar sensors can collect real-time data to construct driving datagraphs based on actual miles (more than twenty million and counting) combined with simulated drives (over twenty billion and increasing). These numbers continue to grow as more cars from automakers such as Fiat Chrysler, Volvo, Jaguar, and Geely get fitted with Waymo technologies and deployed on roads in more cities.

As fusion strategists, we are excited to see Waymo leverage data network effects by partnering with auto manufacturers to demonstrate how today's automobile—the iconic industrial product—becomes tomorrow's fusion product. The Waymo-versus-Tesla competition will be defined partly by their number of physical cars and, more importantly, by the superiority of datagraphs and driving algorithms that make autonomy become real.

Strategists in other industrial sectors must note that, as in the auto sector, adding digital features and functionality and being connected isn't sufficient to make their machines brilliant. Don't forget, digital displays, connectivity through Bluetooth, Wi-Fi and telematics, and remote diagnostics are fast becoming normal features in industrial machines.

It would be an error for the CEOs of industrial giants to perceive the logic of developing fusion products as just another cycle of incrementally introducing new features and functionality that can be delegated to managers responsible for design and manufacturing. Thinking of digital advantage only in terms of engineering excellence in product design and economies of scale in manufacturing and dis-

FIGURE 5-1

Fusion products strategy in the battle of brilliant machines

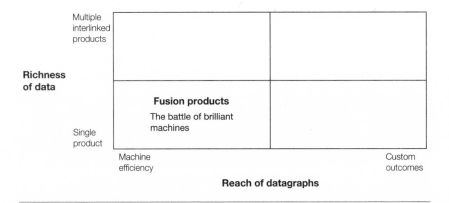

tribution would be limiting. The 2015 observation by GM CEO Mary Barra that the auto industry "is poised for more change in the next five to ten years than it's seen in the past fifty" has already proven true.

The industrials must innovate and develop fusion products by providing digital functionality through sensors, software, and cloud connectivity to collect real-time data on products in use (see the lower-left quadrant in figure 5-1). They must also advance cars' capabilities to collect, store, unify, and analyze real-time data to make fusion products perform more reliably, make them better over time, and develop better generations of future products.

As the fusion products strategy becomes better understood and more prominent in the industrial sector, incumbents must accept more cross-functional changes within the company boundaries and restructure cross-company relationships with suppliers, customers, and partners. The new competitive advantage will be end-to-end visibility, with data traceable across the extended value chain from the products in use back to the suppliers that delivered the modules.

The core ideas of brilliant machines are not limited to cars but apply to many industrial machines that can track and collect real-time data in the field. In the oil and gas industry, high-definition images of different grades of rust on equipment can be used to train models to predict the likelihood and duration of failure, which could help companies like Schlumberger and Halliburton to refine their equipment. At the same time, imaging with seismic data across different oil fields could redefine the exploration economics for Shell, Exxon, and Aramco. In a different context, View, Inc. has developed smart glass, powered by data and AI, that automatically adjusts in response to the sun, increasing access to natural light while minimizing heat and glare. View-designed windows improve the energy efficiency of office buildings while avoiding the need for expensive window shades. In the same industry, Corning could collect detailed images on the drop performance of its latest Gorilla Glass across different smartphones, which could help train its foundation models to derive insights to design future products.

Automobiles, as today's best example of fusion products, foretell a more decisive shift for industrial machines that consists of four essential elements: a product that delivers remote and real-time traceability of its performance across diverse customer settings, yielding data network effects; a business algorithm, powered by AI, that carries out four analyses—descriptive, diagnostic, predictive, and prescriptive—in an integrated manner; utilizing insights from these analyses to deliver personalized value to customers remotely and efficiently; and developing superior products in the next iteration with more-significant opportunities to leverage AI.

Now, let's explore how to implement this approach in practice.

The Journey Ahead

There are four sequential steps to transforming analog products into fusion products; we will use these steps throughout part 2. The first is to *architect* the fusion product; the second is to *organize* the different processes to deploy the product at scale and speed; the third is to *accelerate* the transition road map; and the fourth is to define and refine the mechanisms to *monetize* in order to create, capture, and distribute value. The four-step cycle repeats with rapid feedback.

Architect

How does a fusion product differ from an industrial product? Most industrial companies have designed products using proprietary technologies, materials, and processes. That isn't surprising; they had to make significant investments of time, talent, and capital to develop the science, engineering, and economics of industrial products to operate at the highest levels of performance.

Digital technologies challenge analog assumptions. Fusion products are designed at the intersection of industrial engineering and information sciences. They progressively combine the physical and the digital to create new programmable hardware to enhance the functionality of industrial machines. In addition, they often incorporate modular architectures with software operating systems and interoperable interfaces with other equipment, components, and applications. Architecting the fusion product is a newly emerging discipline, and an ineffective approach is for industrial incumbents to layer sensors and data modules in an ad hoc fashion on analog products. Overlaying digital functionality on an analog design will always underperform versus designing products as fusion-first—with a focus on generating data network effects that make datagraphs reveal more-profound insights and deliver contextual recommendations.

The architecture of fusion products is a departure from a proprietary analog closed architecture; it's an open technology stack incorporating hardware, software, applications, and connectivity. The new design likely resembles a computing architecture more than an industrial product, especially with the focus on tripartite digital twins and data in motion. And it maps how its technology stack interconnects with others within and across industry boundaries.

The shift in the architecture is best seen in the case of automobiles morphing from internal combustion engines to battery electric vehicles. One element in the new architecture is software—the brain that could ultimately run the automobile in place of humans. Mercedes-Benz acknowledged the growing significance of software in the automotive sector while developing the technology stack for its EQS line of electric vehicles. It established an internal team to build its operating system, MB.OS. The company is also exploring ways to incorporate third-party hardware and software, such as Apple's CarPlay, into its vehicles and figuring out how to offer mobility as a service. At the same time, the luxury carmaker chose to tie up with the semiconductor maker Nvidia, which has partnerships with many players in the automobile industry, such as Tier 1 suppliers, sensor manufacturers, automotive research institutions, mapping companies, and digital startups. Nvidia's devices are based on a matrix of configurable logic blocks that are linked through interconnects, can be reprogrammed as designs evolve, and are tied by software to create upgradable products. They will be an integral part of the battery electric vehicle architecture.

The next generation of Mercedes-Benz cars will be fusion products that can be updated and upgraded, built on an electric platform powered by the Nvidia chip and the MB.OS software under its hood. Mercedes has stated that it believes its strength lies in creating operating systems within its own company. It has announced plans to collaborate with Nvidia, which specializes in chipsets, to create a software-defined architecture.[4] As the architecture of the automobile evolves further with greater reliance on AI (as Tesla has already shown), Mercedes and every other major auto incumbent (Volkswagen, BMW, GM, Toyota, Hyundai, and others) must decide on their make-buy-partner strategies not only for the software stack but for other tech layers as well.

Mercedes-Benz should remember that its digital technology stack connects with the driver's smartphone. While Apple's CarPlay integrates with the automobile maker's hardware to control the radio and adjust the climate controls today, it will soon be able to display the speedometer, fuel levels, temperatures, and more on the car's driving screen. Mercedes will have to find ways to interoperate with Apple without losing its ability to collect data in motion. If automakers keep their focus on data network effects that give rise to fleet learning, as Tesla does, they should watchfully welcome software innovations from Apple, Baidu (Apollo), and Google (Android Auto). They must also keep in mind that technological developments in the future could shift the edge that traditional carmakers enjoy relative to digital companies that control the vehicles' brains. That's why industrials must trace the current and future architecture of fusion products—along with those of the compulsory modules and interlinkages—select the areas they want to control and invite partners to complement the vision.

The CEO of Mercedes-Benz, Ola Källenius, is intensely committed to the vision of the automobile as a "software-defined vehicle," but also strongly believes that traditional car manufacturers play a crucial role in integrating various features of modern cars, such as driving, charging, comfort, infotainment, and autonomy. He observed: "If we talk about the two technologies that are driving transformation [in the auto industry], one is the e-drivetrain, and the other is software. In those two domains we have decided we need vertical integration. They are something that we need to own. We need to understand them and own them."[5]

Not surprisingly, Gen AI will influence the automobile and how consumers interact with it. Mercedes-Benz is working with Microsoft to infuse ChatGPT into its infotainment system so that commands can be triggered by the "Hey Mercedes" voice command. While previous-generation voice assistants were limited to predefined tasks and responses, Mercedes is leveraging Microsoft's proficiency with its large language model to significantly improve natural language understanding and continually expand the topics to which it can respond.

Every automaker must develop the necessary expertise to define what it needs to own and how to link the separate domains. Simply making a car digital isn't enough. Using the data generated by the car's performance is essential to continually improving its ability to operate autonomously. Digitizing the vehicle is necessary, but analyzing driving patterns sets it apart. And the progress of Gen AI will compel automakers and other industrial companies to explore areas of differentiation. Fiat, for example, has showcased the Fiat Product Genius, a real person who answers questions from prospective customers in the metaverse, and GM is experimenting with possible future Gen AI assistants.[6] Toyota has gone further by examining Gen AI's role in product design itself.[7] The architecture of the industrial machine and the manufacturing system supporting it are rapidly being reshaped today.

Organize

An analog-digital tech stack introduces new capabilities, such as hardware that's integrated with batteries, software OS and applications, and datagraphs that are analyzed with powerful algorithms. Being an industrial company with a strong background in creating analog products that moves to producing fusion products can be difficult. The architectural advantage will be realized if, and only if, a shared vision unifies the organization, which is the second execution step.

We have lost count of the companies with great ideas that failed because different functions could not work together to recognize the importance of putting a new emphasis on digital competencies. In a postmortem of GE's decade-old initiative to become a digital industrial company, then-chairman Jeffrey Immelt's sober reflection in a 2019 LinkedIn post is a reminder of the three dangers industrials face: underestimating the digital deficit because of outsourcing, the overlapping responsibilities between C-suite functions, and misaligned organizational metrics for measuring digital success.[8]

Mercedes-Benz's vision to be digital-first will require more than setting up a software unit and inking a partnership with Nvidia. MB.OS links vehicles across their powertrain, autonomous driving, infotainment, and body and comfort systems, unifying the organization from end to end. The company is integrating the logic of product, process, and performance twins, each of whose objectives, science, and engineering differs. Standard definitions for error codes in other vehicles operating in various settings must be continually fed into machine-learning algorithms. That will help uncover patterns that link back to past repairs and, wherever possible, can be traced to specific production lines and supplier factories. Unifying data and processes ensures that customer-facing chatbots rely on the same data that production engineers and supply chain executives use to assess supplier performance.

The benefits of seamless end-to-end organizing both internally and externally become even more apparent when you look at a specific case involving auto accidents. Although automakers strive for zero emissions and zero accidents, cars will, unfortunately and inevitably, be involved in accidents. When vehicles equipped with OnStar, an emergency help service, are involved in accidents, GM can identify the severity of the crash with sensors and software but cannot instantaneously link that data with appropriate production lines and specific parts from suppliers. The data exists in different databases, so it is not readily available for machines to query for descriptive and prescriptive analyses.

To come to grips with any accident involving one of its vehicles, Tesla leverages its tripartite twins to pull up multiple types of information: product data from the design stage; process data such as the line, the robots, and the humans that built it; prelaunch test data; and relevant performance data such as the speed, travel direction, seat belt status, and whether Autopilot was engaged. Using its digital network, Tesla links crash-related data to data on all the other Tesla crashes in the past—before emergency vehicles even reach the accident scene—and starts generating hypotheses about the factors that may have caused the latest accident.[9] One of Tesla's key strengths as a producer of fusion products is its ability to study real-time data about its automobiles throughout the entire process, from design to manufacture to use. And as more industrial companies design and deploy machinery with tripartite digital twins, they will be able to take advantage of real-time data that feeds industrial datagraphs.

When leaders understand the power of tripartite twins, they will work to overcome inevitable fragmentation. Deploying digital twins independently will be convenient—for example, delegating product twins to research and development units and design groups; assigning process twins to the supply chain, operations, and service functions; and letting the marketing function deal with performance twins (including service and repairs). The benefits accrue along narrowly defined metrics if such twins are proposed, funded, and operated independently within siloed boundaries. They must be integrated to achieve the full potential of fusion products in the long run.

You may have encountered the term *technical debt* in the software industry, defined as shortcuts that will solve an issue and speed up product development now but that will take more work to fix later.[10] We see a similar idea in the fusion world: *data debt* is when digital twins independently define critical data elements with additional workarounds to integrate and translate the data for deriving key insights. Industrial incumbents will accrue significant data debt if they manage digital twins piecemeal rather than together. Developing a coordinated approach to designing and managing tripartite twins, datagraphs, and algorithms is essential for industrial leaders to create and capture value from fusion products.

If you can minimize your data debt by integrating digital twins, you can maximize your information assets and turn them into business value through powerful algorithms. Recall that datagraph leaders in consumer sectors, such as Netflix with its movie graph and Facebook with its social graph, have accumulated rare, valuable, inimitable information assets that make them distinctive. Information assets will be the critical differentiator as Gen AI gains momentum in industrial settings. And companies must accelerate their road map, which we turn to next.

Accelerate

Compared with smartphones, already used by more than 60 percent of the global population, fusion products in industrial sectors will spread much slower. Most incumbents have a large, global installed base of older industrial products, and the replacement cycle for each is usually counted in decades, especially with machines that show acceptable levels of reliability. The promise of fusion products will attract enthusiasts, while most industrial customers continue to buy, use, and operate familiar industrial products with some digital add-ons. The longer the older machines work, the slower the transition to a fusion future will be. Three steps can accelerate the transition to fusion products.

First, start with business simulations with available data to quantify the likely benefits of speeding up the product replacement road map, including possible market share gains from rivals. If CNH Industrial were to accelerate its development of autonomous tractors, how much could it gain against Caterpillar, John Deere, and Mahindra & Mahindra? Suppose Mahindra could add only sensors and software coupled with telematics capability (without changing their product architecture). Could it defend its market share against digitally aggressive competitors? Add other relevant scenarios to make your simulations reveal attractive customers that may be early enthusiasts. Armed with the results of such simulations, the industrial companies must demonstrate a tangible advantage to incentivize early adopters to embrace and deploy newer-generation fusion products from the outset.

Second, develop a minimum viable fusion product (MVFP) with plug-in capabilities and modules to make current analog products transmit valuable in-use data. Modern vehicles already have onboard diagnostic ports to collect data from electronic control units; tractors and other industrial machines have their equivalents. Deere could do this relatively easily with its JDLink modem functionality for tractors already in use. By adding unique protocols, each industrial company can examine ways to track, collect, and analyze data from "black boxes" that are already built in. While such data was used in the past mostly to analyze failure conditions, industrials can begin to systematically use it as input to animate their datagraphs to develop deeper insights into how their products function under different operating conditions. The purpose of an MVFP is threefold: demonstrate the feasibility of collecting a set of data attributes from the field, ingest the data into datagraphs to carry out relevant analyses, and develop actionable recommendations of value to customers that couldn't be done by themselves. To speed up the shift to fusion products, businesses can use this method to add sensors and software to their existing products, allowing them to transmit data quickly and accurately. This way, companies can also design interfaces that are compatible with their current products.

Third, rapidly convert the installed base. The speed of fusion product deployment is critical to success. Our ask of product designers: work with data scientists to jointly develop a multiyear timeline of conversion from today's state (retrofitting existing machines with telemetry) to designing fusion products from the ground up based on information on the cost and functionality of new digital features on the horizon. Present various options for accelerating the road map so that senior leaders can make informed decisions regarding necessary investments based on a cost-benefit analysis. The faster your installed base of machines becomes fusion products, the greater your ability to differentiate from and win against your erstwhile competitors, which may be stymied by many idiosyncratic constraints.

Fusion products aren't static by definition. Digital technologies—especially sensors, software, and analytics—will constantly change product architectures, reshaping the competitive response. Consider, for instance, blockchain: it could come in handy for mobility services, insurance, supply chain authentication, and the traceability of spare parts. Blockchain promises to accelerate the advent of autonomous driving, with distributed ledgers enabling the pooling of data from vehicle owners, fleet managers, and manufacturers so that the data can be shared across companies in an ecosystem. Toyota is already experimenting with blockchain.[11] We are particularly interested in the likely innovations that could arise from the use of all information concerning vehicle life cycles through end-to-end traceability across the supply chain by recording and sharing information on parts manufacturing, shipping, and delivery. And the power of tripartite digital twins will increase as the automotive blockchain gets built out. That's because of data reliability involving suppliers, dealers, customers, and partners across different geographies. Industrials must understand the likely disruptions and new opportunities from the combinatory innovations at the confluence of such technologies.

A successful product transition road map depends on how the industrial optimizes its "clock speed," to borrow a computing metaphor. It comprises three elements, starting with the *design speed*, or the time to develop the architecture of a fusion product from the ground up and demonstrate a prototype, including the role of its partners. Next is the *development speed*, the time to produce a fusion product. This is about demonstrating not just the feasibility of the architecture but also the required infrastructure, including partners, for manufacturing the number of units needed for assessing financial and technical viability. Last is the *deployment speed*, the time needed to speed up the data network effects to gain an edge. This is the establishment of the steady state where the datagraphs are specified and the algorithms have been trained to develop heuristics on how the product can be remotely serviced.

Monetize

B2B companies price products based on performance and features, but pricing, which is consistently challenging for industrials, will differ in the case of fusion products. That's because they create value for customers mainly by reducing inefficiency in the near term and improving productivity in the long run. Fusion products ensure that a machine's downtime is (close to) zero; catalyze product refinements and upgrades on the fly, based on learnings across different uses by different customers with distinctive datagraphs and algorithms; and develop even-more-innovative products over time. These pockets of value don't exist in the analog world; datagraphs have shifted value creation from the onetime point of sale to every moment of use.

Fusion products offer three monetization options. One is premium pricing, with incumbents able to charge premiums, as Tesla does. Industrials must communicate their features effectively so that customers understand how the fusion product will deliver its value proposition in terms of performance and reliability. In contrast to rivals that can make claims about performance based only on third-party rankings (e.g., J. D. Power ratings) or average historical data, fusion product makers can justify premium prices by using datagraphs and Gen AI to ensure that their offerings operate at performance levels that are superior to those of rivals and have lower operating costs. The information assets created through tripartite twins can help convince price-sensitive business customers whose purchasing criteria may justify premium pricing only with credible evidence.

Another option is performance contracts, which offer guarantees, based on actual data, for different levels of reliability. For business customers such as UPS or Hertz, this option may be attractive when procuring fleets of vehicles. Industrials have usually offered guarantees based on the average reliability of their machines, which they calculate by pooling data on risks, but manufacturers can go one step further. They can back up performance contracts with real-time data, datagraphs, and the capability to fix problems before they arise using digital twins and algorithms.

Finally, another attractive monetization option is using fusion product insights to enter adjacent spaces. Tesla offers better automobile insurance on its vehicles precisely because of its ability to record and analyze the actual driving patterns of individual drivers instead of averaging across drivers clustered into different risk profiles.

The Checklist for the Battle of Brilliant Machines

CEOs and senior industry leaders are concerned about determining if their products will be effective against new technology shifts and competition. They also need help understanding the vast array of digital technologies and how to integrate them into their product designs. Here are three questions to help you know if you are ready for the upcoming battle.

Are your products designed for datagraphs?

Look at your products and the ones you are competing against. Do not excessively focus on digital bells and whistles; methodically assess how your products compare against competitors' in terms of the inherent ability to transmit data in motion. For example, automobile incumbents should look at not just the number of electric vehicles, but how many can track and transmit detailed real-time data such that timely software updates can be pushed over the air. Similarly, tractor companies shouldn't just benchmark telematic functionality to collect data from the machines and how well they update their software remotely. Are you ahead of the pack or behind? What can you learn from other industries that are ahead with fusion products?

Are you leveraging data network effects?

Learning across different settings can give a competitive advantage. Waymo is installing its self-driving software in new and existing cars. This will result in significant data network effects, giving the company an edge over most car manufacturers. In the analog world, higher market share and economies of scale lowered manufacturing costs and conferred advantage. In the fusion world, data network effects will lead to superior performance. How well can you capture these data network effects, as compared with your competitors, to allow your algorithms to derive new insights?

Do you offer differentiated business value?

Fusion products are successful in the market due to their unique benefits, which cannot be matched by competitors that have yet to adopt fusion thinking in designing their machinery. Tripartite twins are a great start but deliver value only when connecting data to results. Advancements in AI have made it possible for industrial algorithms to improve product performance significantly. Automakers such as Ford and GM must go beyond differentiating their cars based on electric architecture and focus on how data and AI drive differentiation. This is relevant for industrial companies in other sectors too. By utilizing high-performance computing in the cloud, they can leverage their tripartite twins to provide data to train their algorithms to enhance their product performance continuously. This approach also enables them to proactively identify and fix any issues before they occur, ensuring that their products outperform those of competitors. Is your value proposition distinctive and appealing to most customers?

. . .

Digitizing or not is no longer a choice for companies making industrial products. But it's not enough to add digital functionality to analog machines. A complete reimagination of the product architecture—from design to manufacture to deployment—is needed to win the battle of brilliant machines. Exploring additional avenues to unlock value with new technologies is only possible with industrial machines infused with digital technologies that reflect the power of data network effects and industrial algorithms. Demonstrating prototypes of new versions of different machines at various industrial conferences is only a start. As Elon Musk mused: "Prototypes are easy; manufacturing is hard." We hasten to add that a real distinctive edge is realized only when industrial companies are able to demonstrate that they possess the expertise to deliver unparalleled value based on data network effects from those machines deployed in the field.

Fusion products are the starting point; they provide the first stage that sets up the industrial company to explore future options. One such option is fusion services, discussed next.

CHAPTER 6

The Race for Remarkable Results

A N AMERICAN GIANT, JOHN DEERE, HAS BEEN PROGRES-sively redesigning industrial equipment—such as tractors, combine harvesters, planters, tillers, sprayers, cutters, scrapers, and loaders—with digital functionality. In the mid-1990s, Deere set up a dedicated digital team that introduced a GPS-steered tractor, giving farmers time back to focus on high-value activities that can't be automated. This innovation enabled the company to tag geospatial locations on every sensor on its vehicles. Armed with GPS-linked sensors, Deere can track the critical steps of agricultural work—planting seeds, fertilizing fields, and harvesting crops—and assess what's working well.

Deere pursued an agritech (agriculture technology) strategy long before the label was coined or had become fashionable. It has over 180 years of experience in manufacturing big iron machines, but increasingly it relies on terabytes of precision data to know its customers' businesses better. Instead of only delivering more equipment or better-performing machines, Deere has been focused on unlocking value by offering analog-digital services that improve the bottom lines of their customers. That represents *fusion services.*

The See & Spray innovation that we profiled in chapter 1—it emerged from Blue River Technology, a company Deere acquired in 2017—isn't an anomaly.[1] In recent years Deere has added sensors to all its machines to collect product-in-use data as farmers worldwide use its equipment. The sensors allow it to analyze the performance and output of its equipment in real time; understand when, where, and why deviations occur; and delve deeper into their causes.

Thus, the company's mental model of a tractor isn't an industrial machine but a cloud-connected computer on wheels. And the dedicated digital team has long been fixated on the best ways of collecting the data from equipment, transferring the data back to headquarters, preparing the data for machine learning with AI, and utilizing insights to help the farmer become more productive and profitable.

Most farmers have access only to data from their farm; each farmer develops heuristics on best practices based on the data they accumulate from their operations and experience, supplemented with tacit knowledge passed from one generation to the next. In contrast, Deere has data across all the farmers who use its equipment and could add value through insights from its data network effects and datagraphs.

By linking all the machines of one kind on a farm, the company's cloud-enabled JDLink system allows Deere to learn from all the machines of the same type across many farms worldwide. Deere has started gathering data at scale; it collects between 10 million and 15 million measurements per second from about 500,000 connected machines on more than 325 million acres of land globally.[2] With all that data fed into its machine-learning algorithms, Deere can begin to systematically develop the processes to prescribe what a farmer should do with authority and confidence.

Because Deere is one of the market leaders, its data network effects are more potent than those of its rivals—which don't (and won't) have access to the data that drives Deere's datagraphs. For an industrial company that has long relied on the scale and scope of its machines, Deere's competitive advantage now shifts to prescriptions based on privileged data and its ability to analyze them at microscopic levels.

That's how the logic that links the descriptive and diagnostic analyses to the predictive and prescriptive analyses becomes its advantage. Deere has steadily gained an edge over rivals by introducing new machines with data collection and communication capabilities and finding ways to retrofit older machines. It has started installing autonomy components in 2024 tractors to enable them to take advantage of future innovations when they become available, and the newer-generation data transmission modems are designed with legacy fleets in mind.

In Deere's case, the hardware and software layers have been combined into an integrated display that serves as a control center for field operations. Its tractors have been fitted with automation for accurate end-of-pass turns in fields, reducing operators' strain and input costs through fewer errors and waste. Deere's all-new 8RX tractor allows farmers to remotely monitor its operations, analyze data in real time, and even operate it autonomously in the future. The company's acquisitions of digital startups have also given it an edge over farm equipment manufacturers that started their digital journeys later. With the acquisition of Bear Flag Robotics in 2021, Deere gained access to autonomous driving technology that's compatible with existing machines—a key advantage.

Deere's See & Spray system is a sign of fusion thinking that's focused on pesticides. Yesterday's best practice in farming—namely, to spray an entire field evenly to tackle weed or pest problems by blanket spraying of pesticides—is progressively reshaped by selectively spraying only on weeds. This innovation is about more than targeted spraying. After passing through a field, the system generates two maps that provide insights to help farmers to manage weeds better. The spraying map shows the percentage of the area on which herbicides were applied on each pass, and a weed pressure map displays the locations of all the weeds in a field. Together, the two maps allow farmers to develop better weed management plans for the future. Only some companies can provide this customized service with access to data, vision AI, and analytic capability. As more sprayers are deployed in more diverse locations, Deere will accumulate unparalleled expertise in weed control.

Farming is about more than killing weeds; it's about managing fertilizers that directly impact farm profitability. Deere's latest product innovation, ExactShot, utilizes sensors and robotics on its machines to accurately distribute fertilizer only where needed, rather than dispensing it continuously along the entire row of seeds. This method reduces up to 60 percent of fertilizer use, increasing business benefits.

A map with fifty billion data points about field conditions and topography from IoT-equipped machines already gives Deere an intelligent nervous system of America's farms and lawns. Over time, data on how seeds, fertilizers, and weeds are managed could help it develop strong causal links of farm profitability on a global basis. Deere's tractor designs are innovative, but the ultimate goal is increasing farm profits, not just machine productivity metrics.

Deere's innovations don't stop there. Its San Francisco laboratory focuses on how best to classify grains using computer vision. Like Tesla's automobile team, Deere's vision team is training its algorithms to learn across contexts, to refine heuristics based on pictures from fields sown with different seeds in different microclimates and varying soil conditions. Seeds produce crops of different qualities depending on the context, which only experienced farmers can identify, but Deere is training its algorithms to do so. Mechanized equipment with computer vision connected to the cloud provides data for the industrial to learn across settings and deliver guidance to farmers for better performance. Through its collaborator program involving promising startups, more avenues to deliver value to customers could open.

The company's digital architecture stack supports its vision to be an agritech leader. The elements include hardware and software, GPS-driven guidance, connectivity back into the operations center, automation to enhance machine IQ with fertilizer and weed management, and, last but not least, autonomy. This digital infrastructure is geared toward delivering fusion services enriched by datagraphs and analytics. To maintain its lead, Deere must interlink its industrial machines, equipment, and AI proficiency to develop a superior detailed ontology of farms' operations. It can deliver unmatched performance to the farmers only with such expertise.

Today's agriculture is data-intensive, and business practices have evolved far beyond almanacs, notebooks, rules, and guidance passed on from generation to generation. Weather and climate AI, built into new applications from startups such as Tomorrow.io, will allow farmers to make more-precise data-driven decisions and to enhance farm profitability. Today's initial innovation on ChatGPT for agriculture—called Norm—answers queries via public data on weather, soil monitoring, and current events. Soon such models, trained on climate data from governmental agencies (such as the National Oceanic and Atmospheric Administration) and the private sector (such as Cargill, Bayer, and Syngenta), could unlock trapped value. This is the future of fusion services.

The Service Paradigm Shifts

Industrials are familiar with service revenue and profit streams because they have traditionally captured as much or more value from services as from analog machines. The development of machines and equipment is expensive; national and regional economic policies have spawned local capital equipment manufacturers in every country. And because the market is competitive, product profit margins are razor-thin. The industrials have counted on services—such as maintenance contracts, performance upgrades, and financing—to swell their coffers, and those services can increase as equipment ages. But right-to-repair initiatives and laws threaten such profit pools. Some industrials offer leasing or subscription-based services, with customers paying only for the output or performance that an incumbent's machines deliver without investing capital in buying them. Such finance-driven services are extensive and lucrative but *aren't* fusion services.

FIGURE 6-1

Fusion services strategy in the race to deliver remarkable results

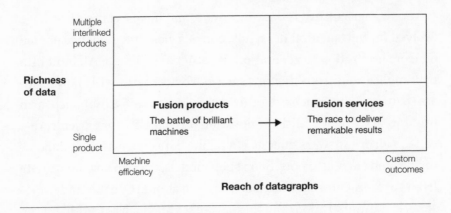

Why? Primarily because those services do not track product-in-use data and take advantage of data network effects. Shown in the original strategy framework in chapter 4 and presented here as figure 6-1, fusion services interlink the company's products with key business processes at customer operations. The tripartite twins extend deeper into customer operations to the extent permitted. Only with this more profound link—earned with trust—can industrials boost customer productivity. The datagraphs expand in scope to include data elements reflecting customers' business goals; the algorithms help predict and prescribe recommendations to enhance business profitability.

The holy grail of industrial services is customization at scale and speed; that is, delivering the right services at the right times at the correct prices to all customers. At present, such is still in its infancy. Experts and consultants make recommendations for improvements after studying how machines work, and incumbents and partners deliver services to keep the equipment running. However, fusion services can create new value with proprietary insights from data network effects and will be able to capture much of the value through personalized algorithms.

Aided by data network effects across diverse conditions and over time, machine-learning algorithms are constantly improving what innovations such as See & Spray and ExactShot can do. Data network effects and algorithms will power what Deere's portfolio of digital-industrial machines will do in the future for their customers. John May, Deere's CEO, says that "machine learning is an important capability for the company's future."[3]

Fusion products and services enhance customer outcomes in fundamentally different ways. Fusion products enable machine uptime to be close to 100 percent, which helps customers spend less on maintenance and, in turn, improves customer profitability. Datagraphs and algorithms have allowed Deere to shift from break-fix (reactive) maintenance to predictive (proactive) maintenance, thus delivering on the value proposition of fusion products. However, Deere has gone further to offer fusion services.

By analyzing data on the operation of See & Spray in different farms, regions, and countries, Deere feeds its AI/ML, which allows it to develop rules for enhancing crop yields. This service isn't about ensuring efficiency regarding machine uptime but about how much See & Spray improves farmers' yields. Using humans to perform a See & Spray service would be costly, time-consuming, and error prone. With fusion services, Deere increases customers' profits by improving the efficiency and effectiveness of their operations. Therefore, the profit pools with fusion services are over and above the profit pools created by fusion products.

To ensure that's possible, industrial companies must design their products so that it's easy to integrate them into customers' operations and thereby uncover novel ways of improving their productivity. To maximize the value they can capture, they must learn to do that without using an army of on-site technicians or hiring service partners, which will be expensive. Instead, the customized recommendations must flow almost automatically from data, datagraphs, and domain expertise supported by algorithms.

Deere's ambition to go from increasing machine efficiency to impacting farm profitability highlights four key aspects of creating fusion services: integrating into customer operations through seamless dataflows, data network effects, and service datagraphs; employing these datagraphs to conduct descriptive, diagnostic, predictive, and prescriptive analyses using AI algorithms; leveraging these algorithms to provide tailored business recommendations to customers swiftly and effectively; and developing future value propositions with deeper service insights into the specifics of customer operations. Let's see how to make it happen in practice.

The Journey to Deliver Fusion Services

Many industrial companies claiming to be service-focused and customer-centric have scant real-time information on how their machines directly drive customer profitability. Although they have access to high-level data that helps them make broad claims about impact, they cannot customize their products to maximize performance for each customer. Their brochures and white papers showcase top-performing examples, but they lack detailed insights on how those in the lower quartiles can improve their standing systematically.

Those industrial companies pursuing the shift to fusion services face internal and external challenges. The internal test is to move away from a sell-first, service-second mindset and toward putting customer outcomes first. Once the rank-and-file engineers and marketers accept this new orientation, the external test is to convince customers (both existing and potential) that the refocus is more than a marketing slogan. Fusion services build on a foundational belief that industrials cannot impact customers' profitability without being deeply embedded into their operations and reorienting internally.

We outline four essential steps for industrial companies to become fusion services leaders. (They're parallel to the four steps for transforming analog products into fusion products, which we discussed in chapter 5.) The first step is *architecting* new services with digital hooks integrated into customer operations. The second step is to *organize* the company's operations from end to end, focusing on customer outcomes. The third step is to *accelerate* the road map to ensure the timely delivery of services at scale. Finally, the fourth step is to *monetize* services in a way that unlocks new value for all contributors fairly and equitably. The four-step cycle repeats with rapid feedback.

Architect

Expanding the scope of fusion services deep into customer operations is a significant challenge, as it requires convincing customers, which typically prefer industrial companies to stay detached from their operations, to participate. Business customers are rightfully more prudent than individuals, who have innocently or ignorantly allowed many companies to link into their daily lives through smartphones and other digital devices and services.

One way to begin the conversation about digital interlinking is to align with a newer business priority, such as sustainability or supply chain resilience. Take, for instance, Unilever's regenerative agriculture principle to "have positive effects on soil health, water and air quality, carbon capture, and biodiversity." Since Unilever prefers to do business with farmers whose business practices are aligned with this principle, Deere, CNH Industrial, Bayer, Cargill, and others could use this new initiative to interconnect their data links to assist farmers in demonstrating their adherence. Global supply chain disruptions have also elevated resilience as a high-priority topic in most industrial sectors, including construction and transportation. Industrials can show how data hooks enable end-to-end visibility and reveal alternative ways to mitigate and manage supply chain risks. For instance, the agriculture and construction company AGCO managed the initial days of the pandemic by aligning with the new priorities of customers to help trigger the flywheel effect—pushing a heavy flywheel to generate momentum until, after a point, it starts spinning faster and faster by itself—to ensure that it could get more customers to interlink.

A second way to earn the right to hook into customers' operations is through education on the value of real-time data. Aided by examples from asset-light settings, industrials could sketch out the service benefits through real-time data analyses. Uber did this in trucking and logistics with an app for carriers that showed real-time data on shipping opportunities and up-front pricing. Such education could be more powerful when supported by simulations based on data from pilot experiments. For example, Deere could take data from See & Spray and project how linking all its equipment through the entire farming cycle could optimize farm yields. CNH is stepping up to show the value of its seamless fusion services (Research → Buy → Plan → Use → Report), which maximize yield and overall farm performance. Bayer's expert agronomists, working alongside data scientists from the Climate Corporation, could convince skeptical customers about the power of datagraphs and visualizations in precision farming.

A third avenue to hook into customers could be to offer a discount on, or subsidy for, fusion services in exchange for proprietary data. Many customers need help getting the flywheel spinning fast enough to gather a critical mass of customer data from which they can derive insights and develop business algorithms. In return for offering services at discounted prices to the early buyers and in the spirit of cocreating new approaches, the industrials could request data that would illuminate and amplify the role of datagraphs and how digital hooks linking their products with their customers' operations will deliver more value for both.

A fourth approach is by demonstrating the industrial's commitment to and conviction about embracing fusion services. Incumbents can improve their chances of getting customers to agree by revealing the digital infrastructure and data-gathering capabilities they've created and the talent they've hired. In addition, they can demonstrate how their customized services will be based not on rigid rules and gut feel but on AI-based analyses of real-time data.

The industrials must demonstrate their capabilities convincingly; the shift to a fusion services strategy redraws the competitive landscape, so they must compete with digital startups that better understand data, systems, and AI. Only by establishing to buyers that their advantages lie in the depth of their domain knowledge, the capability to learn continuously from data, and the ability to provide actionable recommendations for machines in real time will the incumbents win with fusion services.

Organize

After the industrials have gained permission to connect their data feeds to customer operations and have established the foundation, the next step is to ensure that all parts of the organization and external partners agree on how to use the data to provide unique services.

The locus of value creation and value capture shifts from the machines an industrial makes to the services it offers that improve customers' profitability. Yet the internal organization in most companies is stuck in traditional silos with a product (as opposed to a service) mindset. The performance metrics must be based on the buyer's business, not the seller's. Therefore, the industrials' capabilities and knowledge must expand to master the former. To ensure their organizations know more about their customers, the senior leaders pursuing services must consider at least three significant areas for possible changes.

First, the leaders must fundamentally believe and ensure that the organizational structure supports the new strategy focused on redefined services. Deere's new structure, announced in 2020, drives an integrated product road map and related investments to fully meet customer needs.[4] In many incumbent industrial organizations, sales and service functions are separate, reflecting a sell-first, services-second orientation. And most service departments define their mandates and metrics around how their machines perform, not how their services enhance customer productivity. In most cases, they may not know how their machines might be deployed within client operations.

Effective fusion services need sales and services to pull in the same direction, achieve tighter coordination, adopt a single interface for continuous data collection from customer operations, and assess using shared performance metrics.

Extending digital performance twins into customers' operations creates an effective conduit for obtaining richer and fresher data. Deere's comprehensive tech stack supports its entire portfolio of machines in unlocking value for customers through enhanced precision, automation, speed, and efficiency that were previously impossible. In many other settings, the shift to services creates conflicts between different functions and divisions.

Second, CEOs will have to champion the integration of the three types of digital twins beyond their company, as performance twins now extend deeper into customer operations, with a heightened level of emphasis on security and privacy. Tripartite twins focused on how machines impact customer profitability is more powerful and valuable than twins focused on machine performance, as discussed in chapter 5.

Service performance twins will ensure the organization utilizes every opportunity to learn about products in use across customers in various applications and geographies. Suppose a company like Deere or CNH develops a comprehensive and ever-expanding knowledge ontology of critical drivers of customer profitability linked to their machines in use. Doing this will give them an advantage over other industrial companies, similar to how Google's Knowledge Graph gains insights from various search queries. To successfully experiment with Gen AI, industrials must streamline their entire end-to-end processes and have an end-to-end view. This will help them master multimodal knowledge ontology and put it to use to derive recommendations. Gen AI models are of limited value if internal fiefdoms can't be unified.

Third, the effective delivery of fusion services requires the pooling of capabilities from the outside—the strategists must choose their preferred suppliers, vendors, and partners from the start since they will need complementary data sources and technology partners to execute the fusion services strategy. They must develop a road map that indicates where the incumbent plans to make, buy, or partner, and the related resource commitments will show how it plans to interlink customer processes with its own. Thus, the critical step in fusion services is for the organization to shift its focus beyond its machines and equipment and treat every customer's operations as an extension of its own.

Accelerate

How do you effectively ramp up fusion services? This question is essential as industrials must allocate scarce financial and human resources and senior management time to the effort. In doing so, they have to reduce their commitment to other priorities. This reprioritization of resources is always challenging in established companies.

Start with a handful of eager customers to create the minimum viable fusion services (MVFS). This is more than a napkin sketch and slide deck. It's a prototype of how to cocreate the service offering with eager customers, with full details (supported by simulations where necessary) of how data network effects flow into the construction of service datagraphs, how algorithms on such datagraphs yield actionable prescriptions, and how recommendations translate into business benefits. MVFS will reveal valuable insights into the opportunities and challenges of scaling up with these customers. It will start to enumerate what is needed within the service provider unit, the business's buying entity, and the nature of interactions between the two. It will also begin to illuminate the willingness on the part of the customer to share data and test out different monetization mechanisms. This project will reveal ways to complement structured, codified data with semistructured and unstructured data. Valuable lessons are learned even if eager customers turn out to be unwilling to entertain the services on a longer-term basis at the end of the pilot project.

The next phase in the road map is to develop a refined service offering that can be offered to a select group of early enthusiasts. This group, ideally composed of customers of different types across business segments and locations, allows the industrials to test out ways to adapt the core services design to satisfy the needs of other customers. Fusion services are not one-size-fits-all but rather offer modules that can be combined to suit specific needs. Think of the early enthusiasts as a way to understand at detailed levels the different types of hardware and software integrations, the ease of extra data hooks for interoperability, the roles and responsibility for various business outcomes at other customers, and so on. Use this group to identify how rapidly to automate data collection and analyses and the best way to combine machine learning with human expertise.

Based on the results from the second phase, industrials can move to a group of fast followers and then, if all goes well, to a more mainstream offering.

A phased approach allows industrial companies to examine the role of partnerships for data interoperability. Just as cloud computing has lowered the cost of computing, data exchanges—such as those orchestrated by companies including Amazon Web Services, Microsoft, and Snowflake—will make data more accessible. While the data exchanges in sectors such as farming, construction, home building, transportation, and logistics will start with standard data, they will soon expand to provide more-varied and more-valuable data. That will shift the competitive edge to those proficient in analytics and algorithms that deliver actionable recommendations.

Acceleration plans should also recognize the importance of potential alliances or acquisitions. Decades ago, when IBM began its strategic shift from hardware manufacturer to B2B services provider, it didn't have any consulting expertise and needed to buy PwC as a transformation catalyst. In a similar vein, in 2013 Monsanto acquired the Climate Corporation for about $1 billion to combine the acquired company's expertise in agriculture analytics and risk management with Monsanto's R&D capabilities, with the goal of providing farmers with access to more information about the many factors that affect the success of their crops. It was one of the first moves by an industrial company to deliver digital services wrapped around traditional products.

Deere had nearly two decades of internal focus on adding digital features to its tractors before it made a significant acquisition, Blue River Technology. Fully cognizant of the need to accelerate digital competencies, in 2020 it took majority ownership of a battery technology company and acquired a customer service platform (AgriSync). In 2022 it acquired patents and intellectual property rights from a company that specializes in depth sensing and camera-based perception for autonomous vehicles (Light); in 2023 it acquired a precision spraying company (Smart Apply) and a robotic AI company (SparkAI). The CEO and the top team are committed to a combination of alliances, partnerships, and acquisitions to achieve their transformation.

CNH, meanwhile, acquired Raven Industries to accelerate its digital transformation in 2021, and in 2023 it acquired Augmenta, a machine vision company whose proprietary Sense & Act technology competes against Deere's offering.[5] The transformation to fusion services can be organic, but acquisitions and alliances help accelerate it. Industrials should look for attractive candidates for possible acquisition to kick-start the fusion services journey but be mindful of the integration challenges.

Monetize

If industrials expand deeper into customer operations to leverage their data and create new pockets of value, they cannot simply capture all the value for themselves; they must share it with customers fairly and transparently. For example, McKinsey estimates that the digitization of farms could deliver $200 to $800 of value unlocked due to yield uplift and cost savings per acre in U.S. vineyards.[6] Accenture estimates that data-driven decisions could improve farm performance by $55 to $110 per acre, depending on the crop.[7] However, most farmers and industrial buyers aren't persuaded by average performance uplifts that depend on so many factors, many beyond the control of the decision-makers. That's where datagraphs that develop actionable insights come into play.

In the early stages, when customers may need more clarification on the role and benefits of fusion services, consider unbundled pricing, where buyers pay for the fusion product as before, with no additional confounding clauses. Then, they could separately assess if fusion services based on data network effects and recommendations offered by algorithms are valuable. Prudent buyers will examine the relative advantage of third-party service providers versus the industrials with fusion services. It's because pure-play service companies, ones that provide only services and are not tied to any specific product—such as Samsara—have taken advantage of developments in telematics, remote equipment monitoring, and worksite visibility to design and deploy a connected operations cloud capable of delivering competing services. Such pure-play companies can knit together the requisite functionalities without owning the physical equipment. Pure digital service companies add digital links to industrial products at customer locations post hoc, via telematics and software, to unlock customer value and directly compete against services historically provided by Deere, Caterpillar, ABB, and others. That Deere has partnered with Samsara to make its fusion services more compelling is not surprising. It's prudent for industrial buyers to systematically compare the offerings to answer the question: Do fusion services companies, with their integrated tripartite digital twins, offer recommendations that the third-party companies can't?

Bundled pricing, naturally, follows as industrials defend their integrated value proposition, which squarely rests on the veracity of the customer-specific recommendations derived from domain knowledge of products and services across multiple settings. The network effects enable fusion services to shine against challengers that try to develop heuristics based on general rules of thumb. The less complex a business process, the more customers will be willing to let industrials take care of their operations, ensure data integration, and play a value-added role. The more extensive and diverse the customer base to learn from is, the more confident the service recommendations are likely to be. Finally, industrials could also enter into contracts that yield no revenues but give them the right to collect additional data.

In many industries, including agriculture, there's a greater appreciation that digitization could impact business performance. McKinsey's 2020 study of over 100 companies across the agriculture value chain showed that only 30 percent to 40 percent would see positive gains from digitization initiatives.[8] So although just simple digitization through automation will only provide minimal benefits, those that are able to leverage data network effects to deliver personalized recommendations to specific customers would realize higher gains. This is consistent with our own views that the frontier of value from fusion services will be based on datagraphs that accumulate data across different settings (data network effects) and powerful algorithms that develop actionable recommendations tailored to individual customers.

Industrials should pay attention to the role of dealers and distributors in service delivery. Fusion services cannot be delivered remotely using far-flung operations centers and the cloud. Often—and for the foreseeable future—human interventions will be required to fix parts of machines that do not self-diagnose and self-heal. Even Tesla has maintenance centers that come in handy when repairs cannot be done through over-the-air software fixes. Industrials such as Deere, ABB, Caterpillar, and CNH already enjoy a long history of relationships with dealers, contractors, and service providers. These local dealers have tacit knowledge of farming that complements codified data from sensors and satellites. Invite and include them to deliver fusion services and ensure they get a fair share of the new value generated.

The Checklist to Deliver Remarkable Service Results

The ongoing digital changes require CEOs of big companies to consider their business scope systematically. Chapter 5 emphasized the importance of focusing on the digital technology stack to redesign machinery and ensure seamless integration with product datagraphs. Then—and only then—should companies step beyond their boundaries and explore interlinking with customers to make their service datagraphs the lynchpin of future growth.

There are many avenues for providing services to customers in the analog world—authorized repairs, reactive maintenance, extended warranty, managed services, and financial engineering that shifts capital investments to operating expenses. Since those services do not leverage data network effects, they are undifferentiated. Should you pursue fusion services as a strategy? We've outlined three questions for you to consider.

Can our services deliver better customer results with datagraphs?

While services in the industrial age were all about machine uptime, fusion services are about improving customer outcomes through superior expertise and personalized recommendations. You should consider fusion services if you are able to deliver insights on why customer performance is falling short of targets and recommend ways that specific customers could improve their business performance by better utilizing insights from your machines. GE Aviation illustrates this point.

In 2012, when Emirates Airlines noticed that parts on some of its GE-90 engines were deteriorating rapidly, it asked GE Aviation to pull those engines off the aircraft sooner than planned and conduct preventive maintenance; it didn't want any engine failures or longer-than-projected downtimes. The request posed a financial challenge for both seller and buyer; servicing engines more often than planned would increase GE Aviation's costs, while Emirates would need to acquire more engines and spares. In the analog days, GE Aviation would have quietly pulled the engines off the wing, done more maintenance, and absorbed the financial hit.

In a sign of the digital times, GE Aviation turned to GE Software, which used digital twins to model the performance of all the GE-supplied engines in the Emirates fleet. The machines fell into two categories, it found. One set powered short-haul flights from Dubai to the Middle East and South Asia in hot, dry conditions, and the other flew long-haul flights between Dubai and the United States and Western Europe in better conditions. The engines on the short-haul flights were degrading faster than GE had assumed, while those on the long-haul flights were doing so at a slower pace.[9] Using the datagraphs-driven analysis, GE Aviation developed a plan that would benefit both of them through increasing the frequency of maintenance checks on the engines used for short-haul routes. That helped both companies' bottom lines, illustrating the benefits of fusion services.

Do our services combine human expertise with AI?

Caterpillar has been at the forefront of using digital twins to offer data-driven insights to enhance customer outcomes, with ultra-granular forecasting of downtimes and ways to fine-tune automated drilling processes for different customers. But humans play complementary roles: they provide input on how to overlay sensors on existing equipment and how to build next-generation machines capable of transmitting richer data from the field, they design the industrial algorithms that analyze datagraphs, and they ultimately validate and sign off on prescriptions that the algorithms recommended in the initial stage. This augmented intelligence of combining human expertise with AI underlies ABB's approach to service delivery.[10] By designing services as cloud-centric and AI-first, ABB has altered its on-site delivery by human experts into an AI-driven process with human expertise that analyzes problems across settings and arrives at rules and heuristics for tackling them.

You should pursue fusion services if your service delivery combines human expertise and machine intelligence throughout the organization and extends into customer operations.

Is our service knowledge base distinctive?

The significant shift in digitization is not about big data. It's about the evolution in databases from systems of record (what's manufactured where, how, and at what cost; what's sold to whom, where, and at what price) to systems of datagraphs (patterns of how industrial machinery contributes to business outcomes for different customers). Many B2B companies have developed systems for customer relationship management and dealer management, and have integrated customer databases that help calculate the profitability of every customer and compute the probability of customers' not renewing service contracts. Frequently, sales databases are kept separate from data on services provided by dealers and third-party providers.

Look at most automobile insurers' databases: they consist of the names of the insured, their vehicles' models and makes, and the associated insurance claims. Tesla's knowledge base, on the other hand, is made up of data about how each vehicle owner drives their car under Autopilot versus other conditions, which is why it can offer the cheapest automobile insurance with high profitability. Industrial companies in the analog world had meticulous records of what they produced and sold. Those pursuing fusion services (such as Deere, Caterpillar, and ABB) are assembling additional records of how their connected machines perform at different locations. In doing so, they are beginning to appreciate that their knowledge bases for delivering excellent services are separate from and should be more comprehensive than their customer databases. They have accepted that service knowledge bases must be designed to study patterns across customers, contexts, and conditions. They can learn why, when, and where service needs arise and develop rule-based offerings to satisfy all those needs.

The lesson: pursue fusion services if you have moved past siloed databases to create a service knowledge base that continually helps the company and customers improve business outcomes.

. . .

The service frontier is new and exciting for industrial companies. They now have the opportunity to go beyond delivering brilliant machines and potentially working to impact customer outcomes. This doesn't mean you are setting up expensive service centers staffed with humans; it involves extending your digital twins deeper into your customer operations. It implies examining the right conditions to pursue opportunities beyond the machines. It calls for assessing the likelihood of how much value could migrate from products to services and analyzing effective ways to win in this new battleground. It requires recognizing that the competition shifts from the familiar manufacturers of industrial machines to new competitors in the form of third-party service providers.

Deere, for example, must be wary of new, digitally savvy service providers. It's possible that newer players such as Trimble, Farmers Edge, and Granular might try to come between Deere and its customers with new service offerings to disintermediate Deere's long-established business relationships with farmers and other customers. This new competitive threat is due to how these companies could use digital tools to reverse-engineer the knowledge that Deere has accumulated over decades. As Gen AI tools codify knowledge on best practices at a high level, Deere should strive to make its service value proposition distinctive, basing it on data on how its machines could be fine-tuned to extract every additional dollar (or euro, yen, pound, or yuan) of farm productivity. New service value will be unlocked only with the recommendations derived from datagraphs that are not available to those relying on codified general knowledge.

To win the race for remarkable results, industrial giants must rethink their service value propositions beyond those delivered in the analog era, develop differentiated insights, restructure customer relationships, monitor different sets of competitors, and strike new organizational arrangements in extended ecosystems. If those prospects aren't attractive, the industrials have another strategy to consider—integrating machines with complementary products and equipment into coherent systems. And that shifts the competitive battle to a different plane. We will discuss that in the next chapter.

CHAPTER 7

The Showdown of Smart Systems

THE BURJ KHALIFA IN DUBAI—THE TALLEST BUILDING IN THE world—employs numerous systems for ventilation, air conditioning, lighting, water management, parking, storage, elevators, telecommunications, and security. These systems, which operate invisibly in the background, are crucial to maximizing the experience for residents and visitors. When the building opened in 2010, it was considered intelligent because its systems were connected, safe, and energy-efficient, improving its occupants' quality of life.

Ask Honeywell, which supplied many systems for the Burj Khalifa, and the industrial will tell you that its focus is shifting from brick-and-mortar structures to "steel, glass, and click" systems, where digital technologies enable data to travel through the steel, concrete, wood, and glass in which humans live, work, learn, and play. To manage this shift, Honeywell has been equipping all its products—from heating, cooling, and ventilation products to electronic switches, motors, and industrial automation controls—with sensors, software, and connectivity. Deploying them in different industries across countries, Honeywell has gathered heterogeneous data from all its machines.

The ability to integrate different HVAC system components is what attracted the Burj Khalifa team to Honeywell. The company's software enables it to collect and collate real-time field data from the numerous parts of the HVAC system, analyze the data to identify anomalies, and recommend proactive corrective actions. The Burj Khalifa has also relied on Honeywell to deploy intelligent devices to respond to changes in its changing requirements for heating and cooling. With access to real-time data, the skyscraper's team can detect incidents earlier, react faster, and mitigate potential risks. Honeywell's systems have resulted in a 40 percent reduction in total maintenance hours for the Burj Khalifa's mechanical assets while improving their availability to 99.95 percent.[1]

What Honeywell has done for the skyscraper is not a custom project. It was just the start of an experiment where different companies came together to connect their products and services with an agreement to make them interoperable with seamless dataflows to unlock more value. Such systems couldn't be created in the analog age since products were developed and optimized independently; how those products should work with others wasn't part of their design.

The building industry has long operated in three independent and sequential phases: design, build, and operate, with companies controlling each link in the chain with proprietary specifications, operating rules, protocols, and processes. Each company optimized its area of operation, with little coordination between them. Post-construction, to optimize buildings' resource use, comfort, and accessibility, building owners and operators needed to access data from various sources, which proved cumbersome and inefficient. Facility managers determined what problem to fix, when, and to whom to assign the tasks without real-time, end-to-end visibility. And the resolution of issues wasn't recorded in standard ways for others to learn from.

Buildings require dozens of independent technologies, creating complexity, hindering reporting, and making remote building management impossible. Tackling management operations in silos doesn't allow for optimization at a system level or generate learnings across portfolios of buildings. In other words, data network effects have not been developed and used. But expectations are changing. Previously, a building system needed only to sound an alarm when parameters, such as the ambient temperature or the pollution level, exceeded the prescribed limits. Thanks to digital functionality, companies can now understand how buildings operate holistically. By studying how things work together, they can integrate the different pieces and understand how to cost-effectively improve the system's performance.

Because of digital technologies, a new advantage has emerged: data and datagraphs that link all three phases—design, build, and operate. As a result, fusion systems in buildings, in which digital interconnections capture and analyze real-time data, have become feasible. Implementing data-driven insights in real time maximizes buildings' health and improves their sustainability, operations, and occupant experiences. Concrete, steel, and glass are bottom-line assets; data and AI are the new differentiator.

An analysis by McKinsey found that the buildings and construction industry is grappling with the challenges of digitization largely due to the extreme fragmentation of the different parts that must interoperate as a system.[2] And there are few major industrial companies stepping up to the challenge. Like most industrial companies that deliver products from different business units with minimal coordination, Honeywell once operated as a portfolio of businesses with minimal coordination. In 2018 it realized that it could do more by integrating products in a digital world, so it set up Honeywell Connected Enterprise to explore the benefits of systems. Honeywell's potential leadership in this space will be based on its ability to generate unique insights with datagraphs and AI at the system level, not just how its individual parts and subsystems operate.

The Systems Paradigm Shifts

When buildings are designed with an array of sensors—such as those monitoring vision, temperature, and movement—the data they collect

FIGURE 7-1

Fusion systems strategy in the showdown of smart systems

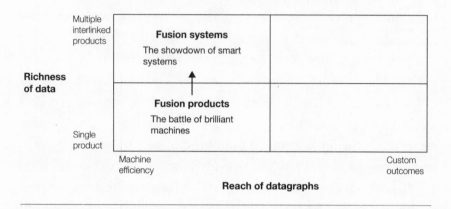

is multimodal and richer than data at the level of individual products. This is shown in the framework introduced in chapter 4, reproduced here as figure 7-1 (see the upper-left box). Instead of connecting a few dozen data points in a building related to independent products—say, energy use and security—fusion systems track and analyze hundreds of thousands of data points across multiple products. Thousands of sensors continuously deliver information about the system's status, the general conditions in the building, and the link to external factors such as the weather. A building twin with a performance data dashboard can then be used to save energy, ensure maximum reliability and security, and step up to new areas of value, such as optimizing the comfort of those in the building. Ultimately, the building twin serves as the single source of truth, a reliable and accessible source of real-time data on the building. This unified view of the building is necessary for Honeywell to construct datagraphs at a system level.

Honeywell and others have started developing AI applications that use 5G cellular technology and sensors to gather real-time data from all the components of a building—including gates, doors, elevators, escalators, lighting, and air conditioning—and analyze it to provide insights into the health of the building and the well-being of the occupants.

Honeywell has been thinking more broadly about business opportunities at a system level by learning across buildings with the data it can amass on many facilities, taking advantage of data network effects. Its technologies operate in ten million buildings—although not all can transmit real-time data back to headquarters. In the not-so-distant future, data from millions of different structures could flow into a single system of datagraphs to help maximize building health and real-world improvements in operations and occupant experience. Insights from such a scale of datagraphs will uncover new ways to add value to customers and differentiate Honeywell from those who haven't yet understood the power of fusion systems.

Fusion systems powered by Gen AI operate not just in the building sector but in transportation, farming, mining, health care, retail, manufacturing, logistics, airlines, and many others that employ equipment made by several companies. For instance, ABB offers integrated systems under the moniker ABB Ability to unlock value that historically may have been trapped in incompatible silos of activities.

It's essential to distinguish fusion systems from systems integration in the analog world, where the integrator is responsible for interconnecting different elements and getting the system to work. Fusion systems' creators must ensure that the system works not just on day one but continually as new parts and functionalities get added. Gen AI is vital for uncovering ways to make the systems perform at higher levels by examining different configurations. The building industry has a rich history with digital tools, such as building information modeling, coordinated global supply chains, and computer-aided design/computer-aided manufacturing. And this industrial sector understands digital twins for design and manufacturing quite well. In our assessment, the success of fusion systems will depend on the degree to which tripartite twins become commonplace beyond individual products.

Fusion systems will generate additional value because efficiency isn't optimized by a single machine but by a system of devices that operate together. Because the weakest elements of the system create disruptions, Honeywell can expand the scope of its datagraphs to predict the failures of subsystems. However, the latter may be made up of machines from many vendors.

Many people believe that the transition to systems is solely a technological change. Rather, it's a strategic shift driven by the capabilities of datagraphs and algorithms. A former chief technology officer at Honeywell said it best by posing an interesting question: "If you build a knowledge graph for a refinery, you can query it to say, 'When was the last accident or gas leak? What happened? What actions were taken?' That's a hugely powerful tool for operations. It's something that can't be done easily today. It requires digital data and connecting data from different sources into one graph." He went on to opine: "Google built the search graph. Facebook built the social graph. At Honeywell, we want to create the industrial building systems knowledge graph."[3] It's doing so at Honeywell Connected Enterprise—the division focused on industrial software and AI—with over 1,800 software engineers, including about 150 data scientists, out of a total headcount of 3,600. The company's vision of creating system-level datagraphs becomes real as Microsoft, Google, and others offer tools to infuse Gen AI with functionality to ingest multiple data types. The main challenge for fusion systems companies is to avoid the traps many fall into by equating big data with data network effects.[4]

The shift to fusion systems is also a movement from digitization at a micro level (a single product from independent companies) to a macro level (multiple related products from different companies spanning various industries). Astute strategists quickly discern that the locus of competition also shifts, from independent fusion products to interdependent fusion systems (seen along the vertical axis of figure 7-1). Such systems optimize value because, as organizational theorist Russell Ackoff said, "A system is not the sum of its parts, but the product of their interactions."[5] And we must add that rich, system-level datagraphs reveal the interactions, and the value is captured through powerful AI algorithms unleashed on those datagraphs.

We use Honeywell as an exemplar to highlight the key facets that any industrialist pursuing fusion systems should consider: designing a system of related products that offer real-time traceability of their performance across diverse customer environments, generating valuable data network effects; integrating multiple data types—text, numbers, sound, and video—to facilitate analytics using advanced AI algorithms at the system level; leveraging these algorithms to provide tailored value to customers remotely and efficiently; and developing future value propositions with deeper system insights that could unlock further trapped value. Let's see how to make that happen.

The Fusion Systems Journey

We have identified four crucial steps that industrial companies should take to become pioneers in fusion systems, as we have for other areas in the previous chapters. The first step is to *architect* new systems with digital hooks across the different products that constitute the system. The second step is to *organize* the company's operations from end to end, to ensure seamless integration across the portfolio of partners that contribute the key products and components that make the system distinctive. The third step is to *accelerate* the road map to ensure the systems are constantly updated to reduce the inefficiency of individual products' operating without an overarching system logic. Finally, the fourth step is to *monetize* systems in a way that unlocks new value for all contributors fairly and equitably. As in previous chapters, the four steps repeat with feedback.

Architect

To stay ahead in its industry, each company must imagine high-level structures of the fusion systems and determine which areas it wants to be involved in. There has been an unmistakable trend for greater integration and interoperability within and across different segments of industrial sectors. The end result is that with digitalization, competition will shift from individual products to interdependent systems.

Therefore, industrial companies must anticipate and comprehend the types and number of systems they may encounter.

A logical question we get asked by industrial companies is, Why should we be concerned with fusion systems when we make products that operate independently? For one simple but important reason: Emergent fusion systems shift the competitive lens. It's no longer product versus product, as in the battle of brilliant machines. Customers are more likely to change their decision-making processes and shift their preferences from products that have distinctive features to products that work together and can integrate with other products to create effective systems. Manufacturers that produce exceptional stand-alone products may face a disadvantage against those that are more appealing due to their compatibility with other products.

Systems can be architected in two ways, and companies should consider both. One is an inside-out approach, with incumbents starting by identifying where and how their products and services will fit into different fusion systems. What's the set of interconnections and likely extensions? What will make the dataflow seamless? Who might be the best partners in such systems? By framing how products relate to and interconnect with each other, incumbents can find their best path to a fusion systems strategy.

For instance, View, Inc. manufactures smart glass in which the tint of the glass can be controlled through software and AI in response to weather or interior temperature. How should the company frame a fusion system in which its glass panes, and the data they capture, are a value-defining part? Can View position itself as a driver of energy efficiency in the design phase of buildings, rather than being chosen as a product supplier during the construction stage? Could it use its fusion product and cloud-native platform to create a fusion system capable of enhancing occupant experiences, increasing employee productivity, and reducing the carbon footprints of buildings? (Similarly, could Deere think beyond its own machines and equipment to develop the fusion architecture of a farm with different subsystems? After all, the frontier vision of precision agriculture will be realized only when the other parts interoperate seamlessly to reduce inefficiencies.)

Another way to design the system is by starting with the desired outcome and working backward, known as the outside-in, future-backward approach. Instead of starting with the current versions of their products, incumbents should look at external trends that could interconnect their offerings into a broader system. What new digital technologies make systems more feasible and economically attractive? For instance, Uber and Lyft were able to create mobility systems only when drivers and riders could see high-resolution maps on smartphones with 5G cellular capabilities. That triggered the shift from transportation as a cottage industry to a global system involving players that are mastering mobility datagraphs and using algorithms. And looking further afield, how could robotaxis redefine personal mobility and logistics systems over the next decade? What complementary parts must be built out to make systems operate without today's complexities of trying to tie together the different parts?

Incumbents must track experiments to show when system-level optimization might become profitable for customers. In 2020 Honeywell conducted a pilot project to showcase the effectiveness of its AI-automated energy optimization system. By collecting data from various HVAC operation components, the system reduced energy expenses by a minimum of 10 percent. Building on such experiments and taking advantage of AI models to redesign its offerings, Honeywell could begin to identify alternative ways to architect the shape of fusion systems in buildings. Powerful AI promises to uncover alternatives for systems design for specific settings in a more streamlined manner.

Organize

To capitalize on the value-creating possibilities that fusion systems offer, the industrials must focus on unifying the different parts so that data flows seamlessly between them and data-based insights guide action. Business leaders must address three issues that together promise to deliver the potential of fusion systems.

First, companies should tap into novel insights at the intersection of critical disciplines. It's time to interlink the data ontology, assumptions, rules, and nomenclatures across different engineering disciplines (civil, structural, mechanical, electrical, plumbing, and energy) that make systems function efficiently. Leaders must combine teams from various fields to make fusion systems work, identifying how traditional disciplines connect with new digital technologies such as sensors, IoT functionality, software, connectivity, data, analytics, and AI. That's how incumbents can generate fresh insights across the frontiers of interdisciplinary thinking.

Second, an incumbent must ensure that all its functions and business units focus on fusion systems. Although intuitively appealing, systems thinking has yet to deliver results because organizations have created functional fiefdoms with distinct responsibilities and performance metrics. That won't be enough when executing a fusion systems strategy. Organizations must contend with the changes to processes, roles, and responsibilities that are necessary when mechanical products and digital technologies work together to identify problems that can be proactively tackled.

Companies will capture value when they pull together functions not just to analyze but also to act. Fusion systems require coordinating closely between functions and units, as well as making trade-offs. For example, a significant investment in system-level digital twins and a reduction in on-site personnel will shift power from the sales function to data analytics. Only some organizations will be able to deal with the resulting tensions. Unifying functions, making cross-functional hires, and creating different cultures will be critical when executing a fusion systems strategy.

Third, CEOs must look beyond the company to suppliers and partners. They cannot define fusion systems' scope only in terms of what they do inside the organization. The dataflows that make fusion systems powerful extend beyond the company, so the trade-offs aren't limited to functions inside the organization. They extend to all the organizations interlinked in creating and operating such systems.

System-level tripartite twins involve different companies, but their priorities and timescales must be aligned to make the system work. A fusion system is only as strong as its weakest link, so executives would likely prefer to control activities inside the organization. In an interconnected world, though, a company cannot control every action and has to rely on intermediaries and markets.

Doing so embodies risk. Every organization should worry about the single point of failure at the intersection of a system's constituent elements. Think, for example, of the failure of the O-ring seals that resulted in the *Challenger* disaster in 1986 or the erosion of the cement at the base of an oil well that led to BP's *Deepwater Horizon* oil spill in 2011. Even during the 2008 financial crisis, the risk undertaken by financial institutions such as AIG and Lehman Brothers seemed acceptable and manageable, but the systemic risk couldn't be contained. Managing risk in individual products is easier than doing it in systems involving external partners. The new requirement for fusion leaders is to step up to the challenge and manage the risks inherent in systems involving people, entities, and institutions in an increasingly data-linked world.

Accelerate

To accelerate the fusion systems journey, strategists will want to understand the role their companies should play in ecosystems as they take shape, evolve, and accelerate. Business ecosystems have gained in prominence as digital and physical domains morph to create new capabilities. In our view, business ecosystems refer to the interconnected networks of organizations—including suppliers, distributors, customers, and competitors—that interact and collaborate to define new ways to create and deliver value. Effective business ecosystems emphasize symbiotic relationships through pooling of complementary resources and capabilities that result in value that might be unattainable when acting independently.

Leaders in fusion systems spot the potential to unlock new value and take on the role of *orchestrators,* which are entities that strategically coordinate and harmonize various interdependent components and subsystems offered by independent entities, ensuring seamless, efficient operations and value creation of the system as a whole.[6] These could be industrial giants such as Deere and Bayer in farming, Honeywell and Siemens in buildings, or Siemens and Schlumberger in the energy sector. They could also be digital companies that see the power of new technologies to draw value away from the players that were leaders in the analog era.

Companies that emerge as orchestrators understand the forces that shape fusion systems and how strategy gets redefined. Orchestrators in industrial systems must build unique playbooks to manage ecosystems, with formal criteria for selecting key partners and providing the right incentives. Without the support of *complementors,* which help make the systems used by the different independent entities that provide pieces to work flawlessly and efficiently, orchestrators may be unable to convince key stakeholders—customers, suppliers, stockholders, and employees—that their vision of digital industrial ecosystems will achieve its full potential.

The orchestrators develop the architecture by which software ties different machinery together as a system with seamless dataflows. Developers write software and create code for new applications only after the systems infrastructure is in place. Those applications are necessary to design ways to track and collect data in motion; only with a robust cloud computing infrastructure can such data be translated into systems datagraphs, and only with AI can those datagraphs be analyzed to arrive at authoritative algorithms.

Mercedes-Benz and Volkswagen, for example, could orchestrate software for their automobiles and invite other manufacturers into their software ecosystems. At the same time, Mercedes and VW could participate in battery-charging ecosystems directed by others. Every automaker must choose to orchestrate or participate in the different stacks. This is not limited to the auto sector but applies to every industrial product—trucks, tractors, trains, buildings, and others—that becomes digital. More importantly, the choice isn't static: the shape of fusion systems will evolve as technology advances further and competitive moves play out.

Systemwide network effects drive fusion systems. They take hold when the adjacent areas are built, making the system more valuable. They effectively unlock compounded value from the other elements in the system. The internet became valuable only when web browsers, email, and other killer apps became available. The smartphone took off only when telecom operators adopted 4G and 5G networks. As cloud computing infrastructure grows more powerful, video streaming has become faster and more easily deployed. And as large language models mature and scale to make Gen AI more mainstream in the coming decade, we will see domain-specific models for the different verticals, with more investments directed to interconnect them to unlock value.[7]

Fusion systems are inherently dynamic. Tripartite digital twins offer new ways to interlink previously independent parts. In doing so, attaining a more holistic, end-to-end understanding of the inner workings of a system is possible. And as new technological developments take shape, the systems will inevitably evolve. AI models introduce new ways to make sense of complex interdependencies through algorithms that are developed at affordable prices and accessible to most companies.

As the momentum for sustainable and regenerative agriculture intensifies, it becomes imperative for industrial agricultural machinery and equipment to seamlessly integrate into various phases of the planting cycle. This involves the judicious use of seeds and fertilizers, tailored to diverse ecological conditions, to promote optimal yield and sustainability.[8] Such systems must be designed, developed, and deployed at different speeds on a massive global scale. The three "clock speeds" outlined in chapter 5 for products—design, development, and deployment—are relevant to systems, except these now involve coordination across multiple companies.

So, one company could emerge as the orchestrator for the design phase of fusion farming systems. At the same time, someone else could step up to orchestrate the development and deployment of such systems. Others may participate in the design phase while aiming to direct the development or deployment phase. Understand the fundamental dynamics that can change not only your perception of the overall role and shape of the system but also how technologies assist in connecting its different parts to generate and capture economic value, along with the roles the various companies play. A static, narrowly defined view of fusion systems will be ineffective.

Monetize

Fusion systems create more value as analog and digital technologies interconnect across companies, and the orchestrator of the system must redistribute that value among the participating players. For example, since the 2007 launch of the iPhone, Apple has captured a sizeable share of the smartphone system with its hardware, software, and services integrated into a coherent strategy. Google uses its Android system to create value in advertising and services, letting hardware manufacturers such as Samsung capture value in devices.

How do fusion systems add value in the industrial setting? Let's explain it using buildings as an example. The architectural design of a high-performance building maximizes the use of daylighting; the engineering design integrates the electric lighting system with the HVAC system to prescribed lighting levels in the different building areas; and the operations design fine-tunes the lighting based on occupancy. Historically, each subsystem was designed independently to reach its focused objective in the analog world. A system-level design unlocks the value trapped in the different silos. In the post-pandemic world of hybrid work, with office buildings not at total capacity, system-level visibility helps adjust lighting and HVAC using occupancy data to minimize the cost of operations and reduce emissions.

As the above example illustrates, systems redefine profits; those architecting the systems are responsible for distributing the value equitably to key constituents, including shareholders and employees. Value creation happens in the innovation phase, and value capture occurs in the implementation phase.

The innovation phase is where the characteristics of new fusion systems are defined, new capabilities are experimented with, and new protocols for engagement between critical players, often across different industries, are specified. It's also when a fusion system is defined in ways that stimulate companies involved in the other parts of the system to innovate alongside the system creator. System-level coordination across multiple entities and periods can be challenging; everyone knows that investments in unknown and unproven offerings are risky. Coordination is difficult at the level of a single product and more so in the case of a system, so mitigating that risk is the biggest driver of value.

Value can be created only in a system with complementary innovations, which, in effect, creates system-wide network effects, as we mentioned earlier. Every smartphone generation needs telecommunications networks designed by equipment manufacturers such as Ericsson, Nokia, and Huawei and operated by telecom service providers such as AT&T, Verizon, Reliance, and Vodafone. Similarly, each element of a fusion system requires signals from other companies that they are willing to pivot from selling products to offering fusion systems. Market leaders must conduct assessments to calculate risk-return trade-offs and de-risk projects by partnering with other companies, as Honeywell recently did with Microsoft and SAP.[9]

Companies must protect innovations through patents. When systems reach a steady state, not every player may have been successful, but they can license their patents and earn some returns for the investments they've already made. Conversely, some innovators may open-source patents, as Tesla has done, to catalyze fusion systems by de-risking them for other players.[10] Qualcomm and Ericsson have relied on licensing contracts to capture the value of their intellectual property through patents; others may be willing to do the same to ensure they get a fair share of the value for their patents. However, when it comes to intellectual property rights involving Gen AI, we are surely in unchartered waters.[11]

While technological advances will throw up ideas about how industrials can create value, they can be realized only when ideas are put into practice at scale. This is the implementation stage, when the players proportionately share spoils. By this time, roles and responsibilities are better defined, with sources of uncertainties resolved. Incumbents can map profit pools to understand the origins of value creation among the fusion system contributors. As business practices evolve alongside the maturing of digital technologies, innovations will shift the profit pools, and the cycle will continue.

The fusion system winners will monetize the value they create through systems integration fees as well as annual charges to connect additional machines. They can also offer software as a service and generate additional revenues by selling fusion systems software to both customers and noncustomers in their industry through onetime license fees, monthly subscriptions, or a pay-as-you-use model.

Prepare for the Showdown of Smart Systems

Fusion products and services exist in various sectors, but fusion systems are emerging. Signs of the role and the benefits of systems are becoming clearer, but the shape and structure of the systems are still being formed. There's little doubt that, over time, competition will shift to the fusion systems level. Three factors are driving that shift.

Data wants to be connected

There have been steady, systematic, and unobtrusive attempts to interconnect and integrate data across domains. Google has started an initiative to construct a system-level Knowledge Graph, connecting about 100 new sources of data elements covering climate, health, food, crops, emissions, and more. It has 3 billion pieces of time series data across 100,000 variables and about 2.9 million geocoded locations.[12] There have been efforts to create more data commons to allow data network effects to be leveraged by different entities.[13] We expect more such initiatives will emerge to assemble and interlink data in areas to jump-start system-level inquiries.

Just as consumer data was codified and connected, industrial data will be digitalized to construct rich datagraphs of industrial equipment, from buildings to farms to supply chains to cities and more. Most industrials are operating at peak efficiency with their products integrated in an ad hoc way. System datagraphs will unlock additional areas of efficiency that lie in the interactions between products. Imagine being alerted to the earliest malfunction in an oil rig based on warning signals elsewhere in the fusion system; the result will be fewer crises.

Digital twins will be everywhere

Another reason for the optimism about fusion systems involves system-level tripartite twins with AI technologies that combine reality visualization, physics-based modeling, and data-driven analytics. We now have the possibility of developing a single source of truth for all virtual datasets that is physically accurate in terms of its digital representation and that obeys the laws of physics. When the three dimensions of tripartite twins are precisely timed and perfectly synced to get real-time data, Gen AI can be a powerful way to develop insights. The twins weren't viable previously because there wasn't powerful enough hardware at the edge and computing power in the cloud. While the need to interlink digital twins across products making up a system was understood, actually linking them wasn't financially feasible except in big projects like the US space program. So, companies optimized at the level of individual products and services. With manifold investments expected to go into the internet of things—linked to Gen AI—over the next decade, digital twins will become omnipresent. That will pave the way for interconnecting digital twins vertically, within supply-and-demand chains, and horizontally, with related applications in industries such as mining and refining.

When digital twins become broader and multimodal, they gain the ability to combine data from sensors in a system that links the physical and digital worlds to produce outcomes that couldn't be previously unlocked. The causes of many problems lie at the intersection of products and scientific disciplines, so the mechanisms for solving them require coordination and integration across domains. System-level digital twins are a powerful way to integrate siloed datasets, help visualize interconnections, and explore iterations of simulations of future scenarios. Many industrial companies have committed to this kind of innovation. Incumbents such as ABB, Arup, Hitachi, Honeywell, IBM, Nvidia, PTC, Schlumberger, and Siemens are on the journey to build multidisciplinary digital twins and help their customers take advantage of this important technological functionality.

The metaverse could be the dark horse

Fusion systems could be more potent because of the potential of the industrial metaverse, which adds boosters to simulation, experimentation, and timely interventions driven by AI-driven analytics. The new frontier will be in industrial settings at the system level. The industrial metaverse, the design and deployment of digital twins, and Gen AI algorithms will result in richer datagraphs that help companies understand how systems operate in different conditions and contexts.

Datagraphs have been used in settings such as music, movies, and shopping without the need for the power of the metaverse. Industrial settings, though, are prime candidates for applying the metaverse. For example, a fluid dynamics simulation for a jet wing may need up to 150 terabytes of data to simulate one second of a real-world scenario.

With technologies from companies such as Amazon and Nvidia, simulations can be effectively carried out in the industrial metaverse.

The industrial metaverse builds on foundation tools and models such as computer-aided design (CAD) and computer-aided manufacturing (CAM), which help conceptualize and create things in the digital realm that companies subsequently manufacture. The metaverse is no different conceptually; it's a digital representation of the physical world.

Going beyond individual objects on CAD/CAM systems, a business can represent a complete digital universe, including elements such as extended supply chains, the deployment of machines at different locations worldwide, and interconnections with other complementary devices in ecosystems. The realm of digital shifts from the use of CAD/CAM in the design-to-manufacture stages to beyond the factory, making real-time performance enhancements in the field. Even recently, industrial companies would have balked at the investments necessary to design and build such innovations—but not anymore, because developments in the price performance of digital technologies make it feasible.

When created, the industrial metaverse will make it possible to collect data on how products interact with humans, devices, and systems to spot extraordinarily complex and dynamic behavior patterns. Previously, the scope of knowledge in most industrial companies was limited to what they designed and built. That will no longer be true, thanks to the metaverse.

. . .

The incumbents' challenge is to ensure that their machines seamlessly integrate with the other parts of customers' supply chains and manufacturing processes as they become more interconnected. Doing that isn't easy. For one thing, the framing of the system matters; that will demarcate the boundaries within which it must operate. However, a rigid definition will restrict incumbents, primarily since the need for systems exists at the intersection of industries.

For another, each system will be affected by the actions of many players across industries. So, CEOs would do well to think beyond the competitors they know. Moreover, companies must fashion their strategies after factoring in systemwide network effects. That means projecting the possible trajectories of technological evolution and deciding when to shift from market segments where technologies are commoditizing to market segments that are taking advantage of emerging technologies.

Most industrial companies have used highly focused strategies to become leaders. They are currently more familiar with analog technologies, so they may need help designing fusion systems to coordinate many disparate machines digitally. They must generate system-level data network effects to create value from fusion systems. They will therefore have to embark on codevelopment strategies to make the right technology choices, choose the correct partners, and use suitable collaboration models.

Ecosystem strategy in the industrial analog world has been based on structures (governance rules, roles, and responsibilities of participants) and processes (how systems will be designed, operated, and adapted). In fusion systems, an added dimension is the focus on dataflows among the players in the ecosystem, as well as how they interconnect with other ecosystems. The point is not just which company is interconnected to which, but the patterns of dataflows from one company to others so that the system can be optimized. That's a leadership challenge that fusion systems leaders must step up to.

We have outlined three different fusion strategies that begin with industrial companies creating fusion products and then extending into fusion services and systems. These are the logical evolution for an industrial company to pursue as inside out extensions. These three strategies may, in many cases, deliver exactly what the customers are asking for. However, there are some instances where the industrial company might be wise to step into the shoes of the customers and understand the shape of solutions they are looking for. That's the final fusion strategy that we discuss next.

CHAPTER 8

The Clash of
Custom Solutions

FUSION PRODUCTS CREATE VALUE BY IMPROVING UPTIME FOR
a company's machines. Fusion services do so by bundling
services with the machines to enhance customer productivity. And fusion systems by ensuring uptime on all the equipment used
by the customer, not just its machines.

Fusion solutions, however, are designed to solve each business
customer's unique problems in their entirety. Unlike the other three
strategies, which start with the manufacturer's machines, fusion solutions start with defining customer problems and then solving them.
Each strategy creates additional pools of value, with fusion solutions
creating the most value. Our framework is dynamic in that all industrials must start with fusion products, but over time they should
migrate to and pursue all four strategies.

Products, services, and systems—even infused with AI—are incomplete solutions to customer problems. Let's briefly return to the
three case studies from previous chapters—mobility, farming, and
buildings—used for those three strategies.

Fusion products are only part of the solution

Cars are an essential element of mobility, but several other pieces must be pulled together to solve the transportation needs of different individuals at different times in different locations.

Ask Tesla, the archetypical fusion products company, about its mobility solution, and the company will say it includes safely utilizing its automobiles through a fully autonomous ride-sharing network—no drivers—and, when desirable, directing customers to public transport options. Tesla's ambitious solution also incorporates optimizing energy consumption by building a fast battery-charging global network and offering in-home charging through a subscription on a fixed price (experimented with in Texas). For Tesla, the mobility solutions space starts with the automobile but extends into energy and sustainability.

Fusion services, too, are only part of the solution

Deciphering the customer's problem illuminates the difference between services that industrial companies offer through their machines and solutions that customers need: both involve being embedded in customer operations. While services and solutions both involve being embedded into customer operations, the scope differs. In services, the scope is limited to the role of machines in enhancing customer performance. In solutions, the scope of problem definition is broader as viewed from the customer point of view. The vantage point in services is narrow, limited to the machines the industrial company offers—such as John Deere's See & Spray and ExactShot. Agricultural equipment (including depreciation and repair) accounts for less than 10 percent of the total input costs for a farmer.[1] For Deere to step up to the fusion solutions frontier and become a leader in precision agriculture, it must improve the productivity of the remaining 90 percent of farmers' input costs with labor, feed, fuel, and livestock as major components.

Offering such solutions won't necessarily call for acquiring physical assets, as most companies did in the industrial era with vertical integration. Now, machinery companies must take an ecosystem approach, define software architecture, and interlink with seed, fertilizer, chemical, weather, and farm insurance companies. Going from fusion services to fusion solutions changes the competitive landscape. Developing solutions will inevitably force Deere into competing with rivals from different sectors: equipment makers such as CNH Industrial and AGCO; component makers like Trimble and Raven Industries; fertilizers and seed companies including Bayer, DuPont, Dow, BASF, and Syngenta; software companies like the Climate Corporation; and, of course, digital giants such as IBM and Alphabet.

And fusion systems are also only part of the solution

Commercial buildings are complex, with automation systems, software and controls, construction and maintenance services, heating and cooling, security, and fire protection services. They are designed, manufactured, delivered, assembled, and maintained by many players but without a unified architecture that interlinks them while in use. The different subsystems interact with humans inside a building, with heating and cooling systems optimizing people's comfort levels, sensors tracking whether a space is being used, and so on.

Instead of simply putting their machines and systems at the core, Honeywell and Siemens should understand how a building is used and then provide a comprehensive solution to ensure that residents are comfortable in every possible way. This kind of thinking will involve more than the systems that provide heating and cooling, and will include factors such as people flows, security, elevator and escalator movements, and the weather. The more comprehensive approach was too complicated and too expensive in the past, but tripartite twins make it more feasible now.

The Solution Paradigm Shifts

In the strategy grid unveiled in chapter 4, industrials start with fusion products and progress logically along both axes. Advancing on the horizontal axis creates deeper integration into customer operations, allowing the industrial to shift from fusion products to fusion services (chapter 6). Progressing on the vertical axis allows the company to interconnect with additional products and peripherals to create fusion systems (chapter 7). Every industrial company should explore those two logical strategy extensions sequentially or simultaneously. Finally, companies should explore whether to develop *fusion solutions strategies* (and enter the upper-right quadrant in figure 8-1).

Tesla or Uber will be able to deliver the most efficient transportation solutions only if they can develop an understanding of the mobility needs of each individual and integrate a set of transportation modes that meet them in an affordable and timely way. So, a solutions company will be proactive rather than reactive, have the right to access and use relevant privileged data to predict what problems must be solved at what time, and assemble the pieces needed to solve them. A taxi or limo company can be easily substituted. Still, a would-be solutions provider

FIGURE 8-1

Fusion solutions strategy in the clash of custom solutions

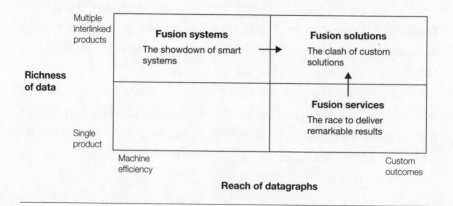

like Tesla or Uber may be less easily replaced by being more integrated into customer operations with preferential access to data. Both companies continually enrich their datagraphs, while taxi or limo companies have different pieces of transactions stuck in siloed databases.

Deere can fine-tune, adapt, and personalize the running of its tractors to bring out maximum efficiency on the individual farm. Still, the richness of its datagraphs is limited to what can be achieved with its machines, equipment, and peripherals. Suppose Deere could expand its set of partnerships with complementary machines and equipment as well as with seed and fertilizer companies. In that case, its datagraphs would get richer, allowing the company to become a trusted solutions provider for customers. The business problems that farmers face are unique; solving them will require pulling together more than one industrial's set of machines. Over time, Deere—as a possible future solutions company—could develop a deeper understanding of how the problems are defined and solved. Its knowledge graphs would get richer and offer more-tailored (and more-practical) ways to solve the issues than what the farmers may be able to do by themselves.

Honeywell's foray from systems into solutions will require a robust, vibrant set of partners for an end-to-end understanding of the entire building life cycle. It's unlikely that a fusion solutions strategy can be architected by a single company. Partners help a solutions company knit together the set of products and systems that match the specific requirements of the customers. In selected cases, this may call for the solutions company to deliver the solutions that best serve what the customers need by not using its own offerings in favor of those from the partners. Thus, orchestrating an ecosystem is critical for developing and delivering fusion solutions.

Where could Gen AI help construct optimal solutions? It can help frame different definitions of problems and generate multiple ideas to solve the problems by leveraging what it has learned across different settings. Gen AI can identify problems and generate options that are missed by humans. At every step, however, humans must interpret the output of Gen AI, modify it appropriately, and make final decisions.

The solutions space—the upper-right quadrant of figure 8-1—must be considered by any industrial if one or more of the following characteristics hold:

- The industrial company has already embarked on a journey to make its products digital with a defined tech stack— programmable hardware, software, applications, and connectivity capable of transmitting real-time data for analysis. This ensures that the fusion products will likely be part of the solution.

- It has already extended industrial products into customer operations with experience in proactively delivering data-driven services. This experience can be further developed to be part of the solution.

- It has demonstrated expertise in integrating products into systems with end-to-end data tracking and analytics. This experience with the system can be expanded into possible solutions.

- It has successfully created and deployed tripartite twins to track data from the field as it's brought back into operations and extended through the supply chain from end to end. This initiative can be developed to track solutions at a granular level.

- It has success in attracting data scientists with expertise in industrial algorithms that jump-start the fusion solutions architecture.

- It has cross-industry expertise in how multiple industrial machines that operate in diverse locations can produce leading products-in-use datagraphs.

- It has experimented with domain-specific AI foundational models to codify and develop insights from its industrial knowledge base, which will be inputs for application algorithms.

An industrial company thinking about fusion solutions should undertake several tasks: interlink deep into customer operations to generate data network effects and construct solutions datagraphs, use those datagraphs to carry out the four-part analyses with algorithms, utilize such algorithms to deliver personalized recommendations to customers, and constantly redefine the core problems to be solved by learning across settings. Let's see how to make it happen in practice.

The Fusion Solutions Journey

Industrial companies should develop a logical plan to assess and execute fusion solutions using four sequential steps, similar to the ones in previous chapters. The first is to *architect* the best possible ways to solve critical business problems. The second is to *organize* the processes across companies to deliver the solutions effectively. The third is to *accelerate* solution delivery at scale and speed across different business problems. The final step is to establish methods to *monetize* the solution by creating, capturing, and distributing value among the companies that contribute unique skills and expertise for solving problems and delivering solutions. And, obviously, the cycle repeats with feedback.

Architect

What problems are you trying to solve? To ensure they are addressing the relevant issues, companies should ask three critical questions before tackling any problems. They should determine how many customers are impacted by the problem; the higher the number, the more attractive the problem is to tackle. The answer should be affirmative. They should also assess whether datagraphs and AI are necessary to address the problem, as solutions that don't require them may not create additional value.

Framing and identifying the problem is critical for architecting the solution; otherwise, companies risk wasting resources, missing opportunities, and pursuing irrelevant initiatives. For instance, automobile companies that perceive the mobility problem as the need to stop using fossil fuels will focus on developing electric and hydrogen fusion vehicles. Companies that identify unreliable vehicles and cumbersome after-sales maintenance as the core problem will likely concentrate on designing fusion products, developing software updates, and deploying them over the air to improve efficiency. Those that see the problem as the high cost of ownership and the low utilization of privately owned automobiles will strive to offer ride-sharing services and write algorithms that match riders with drivers at the point of need. Understanding the customer problem in its entirety, however, leads to fusion solutions.

Fusion solutions become viable when companies aren't just optimizing their current capabilities and resources. One way of figuring that out is to adopt a future-back approach. Companies can use *backcasting*, in which desired conditions are envisioned and then actions are defined and taken to attain those conditions, rather than merely taking steps that are a continuation of the present ones. Backcasting is similar to envisioning, but its purpose isn't to determine the future; the purpose is to imagine many possible futures and understand their implications, identify the preferable ones, and identify the steps needed to bring about those futures.

For instance, if a company is interested in solving the many problems associated with urban transportation—people's mobility challenges, cities' traffic congestion issues, environmental pollution problems, and more—it would be taking on a complex, multidimensional problem that only fusion technologies can solve. The company would have to work back from an ideal future; a higher-order framing of the problem from the outside will solve the challenge by forcing incumbents to step out of their past and into the future.

A would-be transportation solutions leader must ask: Should we allow a single passenger to drive a vehicle designed for four people? Should logistics companies rely on vehicles intended for transporting people? What will the economic and environmental impacts be if purpose-built cars are deployed? Should we use human drivers or autonomously driven vehicles? What changes will roads need to accelerate the deployment of autonomous cars? How will mass transit systems have to adapt? What about fuel, service, repairs, and parking?

It isn't as far-fetched as it may seem; many industrials are reimagining their futures in purposeful ways. Companies in the agriculture sector are trying to find ways to sustainably feed the whole world. Construction and building companies are trying to architect buildings to house more people comfortably, sustainably, and cost-effectively. Health care companies are hoping to cure illness and disease at every stage. In the remainder of this decade, fusion solutions will emerge in many industrial businesses, with the early movers developing end-to-end fusion solutions.

Many incumbents will tackle problems with solutions that emerge from the intersections of digital thinking and scientific disciplines. Consider, for example, the science of biology, the study of living things and life. Altering the genetic code changes biological systems, which has become possible only because of digital technologies. Indeed, biology is being reframed with technologies such as gene sequencing, gene editing (CRISPR/Cas9), and synthetic biology. Scientists can read, edit, and write new DNA; digital technologies render it into data. That's why incumbents in a range of industries—from health, beauty, and medical devices to electronics, pharmaceuticals, and food chemicals to even mining, electricity, and construction—are examining their roles in the synthetic biology business.

Architecting solutions is helped by looking at the problem from the customer's perspective—why would customers need industrial companies to provide the answers? Creating solutions on a case-by-case basis is expensive, and most industrial buyers would not find such an approach interesting. Instead, customers will choose solutions providers for their expertise in *assembling* the best solutions from all the available products, services, and systems, based on their mastery of data network effects and distinct algorithms.

Organize

Solutions can be delivered not by standard products, services, or systems but by their interconnections with complementary products, services, and systems. That means the organizing logic will be critical to delivering the solutions. The advancement of precision agriculture, intelligent buildings, personalized health care, sustainable transportation, and smart homes will not be achieved solely by separate companies creating new products. Instead, it will come from integrating these products with other, complementary parts to form effective solutions.

The fusion solutions company must act as a provider and a consultant. For example, Honeywell designs buildings using existing modules and subsystems and adds necessary features to meet its customers' needs. The company must be skilled at collaborating with various partners to ensure that the solution is tailored and addresses the problem at hand.

Industrials will develop customized solutions by combining humans and technologies. The fusion solutions company must develop the digital skills to knit together products, services, and systems that it has under its control alongside its partners. The digitals (the startups) have the luxury of developing the solutions without using or adapting existing parts. The industrials need to calibrate the performance gap—how well their solutions stack up against competitors who do not have their degree of constraints and operate more freely to develop the best solutions for the customers.

Currently, companies develop solutions on a case-by-case basis with human experts on the ground. In the future, solutions will rest on integrated dataflows and the expertise accumulated from data network effects across different settings. Developing digital technologies that follow the customer life cycle is critical to increasing the value of relationships between industrial companies and their customers.

Accelerate

To accelerate progress on fusion solutions, providers must develop robust digital tools to efficiently provide customized solutions on a large scale. It is essential to always watch for advancing technologies that can be combined to create personalized solutions that can adapt to changing problems. Look for technologies that are maturing and converging to achieve the most effective integration of different pieces. This approach ensures that past methods of problem-solving do not limit future solutions.

CEOs must choose which new capabilities should be developed inside the organization and which ones they will need to partner with digital startups and giants for. This process will trigger the reprioritization of investments in people, procedures, and policies. Innovations in one domain will fuel creative ways to solve problems in other fields. For example, Tesla's use of visual computing for self-driving technologies has inspired Amazon's creation of cashierless stores.[2]

Using fusion technologies to solve problems requires agility and adaptation. Leaders must embrace digital technologies, delve deeper to understand their potential, and create a culture of curiosity so that digital innovations aren't limited in their applications. They must allow experimentation, which will enable them to know when technologies will be ready for adoption and what complementary innovations will be necessary to apply them. The core competency of a fusion solutions company isn't using rules and crafting solutions that work for extended periods; it's looking for inspiration from different domains so that it can continue solving problems more effectively.

Most significant problems aren't static, and fusion strategies can't be either. By accessing real-time data about how solutions work in different settings, a fusion solutions provider can refine them to become more efficient and effective. Urban congestion isn't a new problem, for example. However, the options to economically transport people and goods with minimal environmental impact are more varied than before—and even better solutions could be possible.

Fusion solutions are inherently dynamic, with access to real-time data on how different solutions work in distinct settings. By assembling data network effects over time, the fusion solutions company can constantly reframe the problem, fine-tuning its understanding of how to arrive at the best solution. The company must earn the right to embed deep into customers' operations to be effective.

Monetize

Because the role of customers and partners in cocreating value is most significant when fusion solution strategies are used, industrials must share that value with customers and partners.

Customers are often willing to pay more for solutions than for products. The industrials can monetize fusion solutions through outcomes-based contracts and profit-sharing agreements. Some industrials are already experimenting with self-monitoring services that replenish themselves automatically; with subscription models, which charge a regular, time-based fee for solutions; and with as-a-solution businesses, which provide solutions tailored to the customer's needs. France's Alstom ensures that the trains it makes meet customers' needs 24-7 with its Train Life Services business, and incurs financial penalties for breakdowns, particularly during peak hours. Germany's Kaeser Kompressoren no longer sells cylinders of air; it sells air compression as a service, using digital technologies to monitor its machines' use remotely. And Holland's Philips sells lighting solutions, rather than LED bulbs, to customers such as Amsterdam's Schiphol Airport.

Let us consider how best to create maximum value from fusion solutions. When a solutions company brings its cross-industry expertise and datagraphs to bear on how different pieces should fit together to maximize value, it can fully comprehend and, if needed, redefine the problem. In turn, it works with richer data in motion that feeds its datagraphs; the data is of greater scale and scope regarding the number and diversity of settings. That detail provides the basis for developing solutions unavailable to competitors with limited scale and scope of operations. And as the industrial company increasingly works with more partners, it is able to refine its fusion solutions to unlock more value.

Value creation stems from continually pooling expertise. Solutions companies can learn about the specifics of each customer only from the datagraphs derived from the set of machines in use at customers' locations. They build on this expertise directly or indirectly by partnering with other companies and can expand their scope from being systems integrators or service providers. They must build on their knowledge about how systems as configured are designed to work and complement it with data from partners that are more deeply embedded in client operations.

The fusion solutions provider must be seen as an innovator, possessing capabilities at the nexus of scientific disciplines and digital technology. Only as an innovator can it attract promising partners; an industrial seen as a laggard will not gain the support of innovators. A solutions company's credibility will be assessed through the lens of the partners it has been able to collaborate with. Still, the best companies pursuing products, services, and systems strategies won't want to work with B-list solutions companies.

In addition, it is essential to be regarded as a trusted ally that understands the roles played by partners. Partners often need to understand that their expertise will be appropriated through reverse engineering without attribution or compensation. Demonstrating an unwavering commitment to respecting partners' contributions and ensuring that each gets a fair share is critical. Since a partner may play a different role for each customer, the solutions company must communicate the rationale for distributing value. Trust also plays a vital role because the fusion solutions company will be at the center of dataflows from partners that could be competitors in highly meshed ecosystems.

Solutions providers must be fair in resolving conflicts and communicating ecosystem rules. They may have focused on data governance in the past, but it extends further into customers and partners when delivering solutions. Elevating the importance of privacy and security as drivers of value creation and capture is paramount. When fusion solutions depend on the coordinated actions of many companies, the weakest link contributes to underperformance. If that happens, the fusion solutions company must be perceived as an honest broker and a fair arbitrator to ensure that value is enhanced, not destroyed.

Preparing for the Clash of Customized Solutions

Of the four fusion strategies, fusion solutions may be more appealing to new entrants that do not have a background in machinery design and manufacturing. They can bring their fresh perspectives to frame problems and use digital technologies, including recent developments in AI and ML, to develop alternative ways to solve the issues, and then rely on products and systems to pull together what's needed. These companies have the advantage of being unbiased since they are not affiliated with any corporate entity that might influence their recommendations. Therefore, they are free to provide the most effective solutions to the customer's problem.

Consulting companies may find fusion solutions appealing. They excel at gathering best practices from past experiences to create tailored strategic directions and recommendations for their clients. But they have relied on intelligent humans without access to industrial companies' real-time, product-in-use data and data network effects. They could, though, partner to deliver solutions, as Accenture has recently done with its Industry X initiative. The firm's claim is ambitious:

> We use the combined power of data and digital to reimagine the products you make and how you make them. With digital intelligence connecting every point along the way, we will work with you using data and technologies such as AR/VR, cloud, AI, 5G, robotics, and digital twins to embed greater resilience, productivity, and sustainability into your core operations. And create

new, hyper-personalized experiences and intelligent products and services."[3]

While we haven't seen proof of the successful execution of this idea, it is instructive to recognize that the competitive battle in fusion solutions will be between traditional industry leaders and new entrants with digital competencies.

Should your company choose to play on this battlefield? Three factors will shape the competitive tussles and influence the decision to move into fusion solutions.

The growing size of the solutions gap

Every industry sector has a solutions gap: the difference between what customers need and what the best offers provide. Most industries have reached a point where their current products, services, and systems can no longer increase business value. Unless new approaches that reflect the core ideas of fusion are implemented, the solutions gap will continue to widen. It's untenable to solve urban congestion and deliver personalized transportation solutions by having more cars on the road. It's unsustainable to feed the world's eight-billion-plus people with traditional approaches to agriculture and farming. It's not possible to make health care more affordable without fusing digital functionality. It's not viable to design healthy, sustainable urban living without reimagining how structures are designed from the ground up, with different philosophies and approaches. If the current players cannot meet customers' needs, a larger and more significant solutions gap will bring in new competitors with the necessary capabilities.

The portability of cross-industry solutions

Fusion solutions can be financially lucrative by exploring solutions from related industries. For instance, how can successful practices from urban transportation be implemented in farming? How can the expertise of companies like Waymo or Cruise in autonomous cars be applied to mining?

One team at Google's Mineral project has been on a quest to build new software and hardware tools to bring together diverse sources of information that until now were too complex or too overwhelming to be valuable and actionable.[4] To begin with, the team collected information that was already available about the environmental conditions in the field. This included data on soil, weather, and crop history. The team also used a prototype plant rover to gather new data on how the plants in the area grew and adapted to their environment. The rover rolled through the fields, inspecting crops up close. Data was collected for training machine-learning algorithms using a plant rover that explored strawberry fields in California and soybean fields in Illinois. The algorithms were trained with high-quality images of plants, berries, and beans.

Over two years, the team has analyzed a range of crops—such as melons, berries, lettuce, oilseeds, oats, and barley—from planting to harvesting. By combining the imagery gathered by the rover with other datasets such as satellite imagery, weather data, and soil information, the team has been able to create a comprehensive picture of what's happening in the field and use machine learning to identify patterns and valuable insights into how plants grow and interact with their environment. It may appear that Mineral has been developing capabilities similar to those that Deere has acquired with Blue River Technologies. However, Mineral differs because it can access a broader cross-section of AI, computer vision, and machine-learning innovations than Deere can. That allows Google to use digital approaches to solving problems across industries.

The pull of different ecosystems

Solutions ecosystems will emerge at two poles. One will be digitally led; companies with digital competencies (such as Accenture or Mineral) will seek to partner with traditional industrial companies to acquire complementary domain expertise. The other will be discipline-led; industrial leaders with disciplinary knowledge (Deere in farming, Honeywell in construction and aerospace, Caterpillar in mining, etc.) will seek to partner with digital companies (such as Nvidia, Taiwan Semiconductor Manufacturing Company, Microsoft, or Amazon Web Services) to access complementary expertise to solve problems. Watching such ecosystems take shape and gain momentum in different sectors—as early warning signals of likely value shifts—is essential.

. . .

We've outlined four key battlegrounds that industrial companies will find themselves in as the global economy becomes increasingly digitized. Suppose they continue on the path established in the analog era. In that case, they will face competitive challenges from rivals that recognize the need for fusion products to win the battle of brilliant machines, such as Tesla in the automotive sector. Thus, industrial companies must embrace digital engineering to define their machine architecture or risk falling behind. They must recognize that staying still exposes them to new competitors with new competencies. Table 8-1 is a summary comparison of the four execution steps across the four fusion strategies.

However, fusion products capture only a small portion of the untapped value as the fusion frontier opens new possibilities along the two axes. At this point, industrial leaders have two options: delve deeper into customer operations to win the race for exceptional results and become an integral driver of enhanced customer profitability or explore alternative routes into systems.

The most effective approach to winning the race for fusion systems is through the dynamic interplay of datagraphs and tripartite digital twins that are deeply embedded in customer operations. Failing to achieve this will open the door for third-party service providers to seize opportunities.

TABLE 8-1

Steps in the execution of the four fusion strategies

Execution step	Fusion products	Fusion services	Fusion systems	Fusion solutions
Architect the offering	Design the digital industrial product that is guided by datagraphs and algorithms to compete against analog machines.	Design the links to interconnect into customer operations to enhance customer outcomes.	Design the systems so that different machines operate seamlessly, even if manufactured by different industrial companies. Track and assess data on system-level performance.	Offer solutions by integrating products and systems and then adding what's needed to solve customer problems. Data network effects across multiple settings create an advantage.
Organize to deliver value	Unify the organization and partners around tripartite digital twins. Create the capability to convert data into business value.	Extend tripartite digital twins into customer operations to deliver actionable recommendations that increase customer productivity.	Develop system-level thinking to interconnect different machines. Decide on the orchestration and participation roles.	Use the best of humans and AI to frame and solve problems; adopt an outside-in perspective and future-back orientation.
Accelerate the road map	Add sensors and software to existing machines, and then progressively replace the installed base with fusion products.	Start with enthusiastic customers who foresee the value of interoperability. Apply the lessons learned to a broader set of customers.	Create subsystems around products and expand the scope to unlock system-level benefits.	Start with today's high-value problems that can be solved with available technologies, and then develop a road map for future solutions delivery.
Monetize for value creation and capture	Increase reliability and reduce the risk of machine downtime for customers.	Unlock new ways to enhance customer productivity through datagraphs and algorithms.	Use seamless systems to unlock value that was previously trapped within siloed functions and individual companies.	Customize solutions to unlock value that otherwise would be lost due to incompatible offerings with narrow problem scope.

The showdown of intelligent systems is relevant for every industrial company as it continually assesses how to connect with different systems or take charge of architecting and managing dataflows during system operations. Companies like Honeywell will find themselves increasingly entwined in multiple overlapping systems as they develop a comprehensive, end-to-end view of their products and systems. This battle will play out across industries as they digitalize and interconnect with adjacent sectors.

The final battle centers on customization via integrating products and systems to address specific customer needs based on accumulated insights over time. Industrials with in-depth knowledge of their machines and systems will compete against those acting as customer agents. Winning this battle will require profound insights and mastery of AI tools.

The four battlegrounds represent different value vectors. Both industrial and digital companies are positioned to seize shares of the $75 trillion addressable opportunity in asset-heavy sectors. Generative AI, combined with deep domain knowledge, promises to deliver a more comprehensive, multidisciplinary approach to framing and solving problems in sectors including personalized transportation, smart farming, home comfort, and sustainable energy. Ultimately, the power of strategic innovations will redistribute value among those with new capabilities, which can enter into new relationships.

In this part, we have outlined not only the four strategies but also the dynamics of evolution. Every industrial company must consider its present strategy and simultaneously look at evolutionary paths to seize new opportunities. The focus now shifts to the leadership challenges of making fusion an integral part of strategy formulation and execution. We offer a set of principles and practices to help leaders get started on this important journey in the concluding part.

PART THREE

CONQUERING THE FUSION FRONTIER

CHAPTER 9

Fusion Principles and Practices

FAST-FORWARD TO 2037. IT'S NOT FAR-FETCHED TO IMAGINE that the talk of the town square (the digital and global one, of course) is how John Deere, the American agricultural giant established exactly two hundred years back, has remade itself into one of the winners in farming and food. Not many companies have celebrated two centuries without being acquired or morphed into some other corporate entity.

It started soon after John May, twenty-three years after joining the company, became chairman and CEO in 2020—only the tenth CEO in Deere's history. He announced that Deere's strategy would not be just about machines. The new "smart industrial" strategy aimed to transform agriculture and construction.

What caught people's attention was the company's focus on the entire technology stack to enable its machines to be more innovative, precise, and productive. Its approach was to combine the technology stack and life-cycle solutions. Equally important was its focus on continually adding value throughout the life of its equipment to minimize costs and maximize uptime. The company's imagination extended beyond industrial machinery to include hardware, guidance, connectivity, machine IQ, and autonomy. Its business vision focused on delivering solutions to its customers—the North Star of the fusion strategy grid. Its directive in 2023: "We're directing the power of our enterprise to deliver intelligent, connected machines and applications that will revolutionize our customers' businesses, delivering value across the full lifecycle of our products in ways that are sustainable for all."[1] Its updated tagline, "We run so life can leap forward," reflected Deere's ambition to reinvent itself for the fusion future.

May's vision set the company on its future course. In the early 2020s, it started to prepare for the upcoming battles against traditional and new competitors, recognizing that its new competencies would combine steel and silicon, physical and digital, and human and AI. Deere reasoned that if it could become the trusted partner for the farmers along the entire farming life cycle—prepare, plant, protect, harvest, and manage—it could unlock an additional $40 per acre of economic value.[2] Once the value is unlocked, the distribution of this value depends on the nature of relationships between the industrial companies and the buyer (namely, the farmer). To become the trusted partner, Deere needed to combine its expertise in industrial machinery with insights from datagraphs and algorithms. It needed to use the data network effects of its millions of machines and pieces of equipment operating in the field. Then if the company successfully unlocked the additional value, it could legitimately claim a fair share.

Deere embarked on a journey to become more deeply integrated into customer operations. It set a goal of 500 million engaged acres (defined as acres with at least one operation digitally tracked by the customer in Deere's digital platform within a twelve-month period), with 50 percent of those highly engaged (acres with multiple operations digitally tracked by the customer in Deere's platform within a one-month period), and at least 1.5 million connected machines by 2026.[3] It had already been investing in designing connectivity since the 2010s. By focusing on the data to power farming, Deere's solutions would "empower customers to achieve their aspirations, to do their jobs more precisely and productively through advanced technology as well as make better decisions based on data."[4]

Will history ultimately record how Deere redefined tractors and industrial machinery at the interconnection of steel and silicon to remake itself for its third century? Competition, of course, will have a significant say in how well Deere succeeds at the nexus of its own performance and customer productivity. Analysts and observers will document how precisely Deere taps into advances in science to push the frontier of sustainability without sacrificing profitability. Will Deere be the poster child of digital industrial reinvention, or will other incumbents make up ground on the lead that Deere had built in 2024?

Though it is impossible to predict the future, we are sure the winners will embrace some—if not all—of the principles and practices we outline below. The future competitive landscape for industrials will be different—uncharted and unfamiliar. The battlegrounds will be different, with new competitors with a new set of competencies fit for the fusion future. If Deere and other industrial incumbents are to win, they will need a new strategy playbook. They must urgently assess the relevance of their existing competencies, discard outmoded practices, and embrace the logic of the digital era. And they must adopt new principles and employ new techniques.

Principle One: Unlock New Business Value Across Multiple Stages

Fusion integrates advanced scientific knowledge with cutting-edge digital technology, transforming competitive battles, creating new avenues to unlock value, and offering novel methods for capturing value. Analog-era practices had limits on the upper bound of value creation, as they were restricted by rigid business boundaries, functional confines, and organizational borders. Now, forward-looking senior leaders readily see the sparks of isolated ideas that could unlock hidden value but recognize that it will likely happen over several stages. Multiple technologies must mature and converge to unlock the bulk of the trapped value. We expect industries and segments will see diverse trajectories: what worked for personal mobility may not work for commercial logistics or farming; what might work in the United States may not directly translate to other parts of the world. Although digital disruption is poised to destabilize every industry within the next decade or two, the routes to value redistribution remain uncharted. To navigate this terrain, it is imperative to establish and enhance two analytical practices.

Let hundreds of experiments bloom

How best to unlock value remains undefined and unknown during this uncertain period, calling for disciplined strategic experimentation. Deere aims to unlock, on average, a $40-per-acre productivity gain, but the precise means and mechanisms to achieve this still need to be discovered—and they are likely to be very different for customers facing diverse conditions. Deere must meticulously experiment, combining digital technology with organizational processes to develop specific routines that unlock business value in different customer settings. These experiments will enable it to create a road map of sensors, software, and peripherals needed to enhance the performance of existing machinery while developing insights to design next-generation equipment.

Experiments help companies refine their current practices and adapt for the future across different time horizons. The challenge lies in finding success in today's battles (horizon one: one to three years) while preparing for future battlegrounds (horizon three: seven-plus years). Significant business challenges emerge, though, in the intermediate time horizon (horizon two: three to seven years). CEOs must decide when to abandon traditional practices and how rapidly to adopt new practices that are likely to form future business foundations. For Deere, horizon-two decisions involve balancing the evolution of its machines with digital integration inside customer operations, including interconnections with non-Deere machines and equipment that make up farming systems.

Deere's success in its smart industrial strategy depends on preserving crucial capabilities for value creation and capture in horizon one while shedding those likely to be less relevant for horizon three.[5] It must accurately identify the timing of future breakpoints—instances where past best practices may lose their relevance. Additionally, it must judiciously determine which practices to abandon, ensuring that the risk of forfeiting valuable skills and knowledge is minimized. By designing coordinated experiments, including data-driven simulations across the three horizons, Deere can identify and reallocate unproductive resources from obsolete business models to those that unlock new business value.

Be the best at backcasting

Forecasting, while straightforward, can be limiting as it projects from general information and tends to perpetuate existing biases—for example, a tendency to overestimate the effect of a technology in the short run and underestimate the impact in the long run.[6] Additionally, forecasting is most useful under predictable conditions. In contrast, backcasting is more challenging but essential when companies face discontinuous and nonlinear shifts in technology, customers, and competitors; discontinuity disrupts established pockets of value. Backcasting also helps companies determine where business value could be created and captured by working backward from different plausible futures rather than projecting forward from the present.

Working back from 2037, Deere should take into account the role of electrification of its machines. It's very likely that the popularity of electric cars and trucks will spill over into tractors and construction equipment. One, autonomous driving systems and the electrification of cars could directly impact the architecture of tractors and construction equipment. Two, electrification could indirectly reduce the demand for corn, a key ingredient in ethanol, which powers traditional internal combustion engines. If demand for ethanol slows over the next decade or two, how could Deere help farmers that grow corn manage their orderly transition to other crops? This is more than Deere might do as an industrial machinery manufacturer, but it is undoubtedly something it must do as a solutions company. Backcasting reveals connections across weak signals across time horizons, enabling a more comprehensive understanding of future business landscapes, one shaped by the convergence of multiple trends and technologies.

Adopting an outside-in perspective, backcasting facilitates a deeper comprehension of the intersection of emerging technologies and evolving customer needs to unlock hidden value. Deere must track developments in adjacent areas, such as seeds and fertilizers, that could become relevant to and influence the suite of sensors and software on its machines. This backcasting approach can help a company identify value stream breakpoints, focusing on profit pool shifts rather than technological advancements. Mapping the changes in profit pools offers invaluable insights into players that could both emerge as crucial business partners and reorder the distribution and sharing of value that digital shifts would unlock.

To make backcasting effective, companies must transition from considering a general description of the future to having a specific vision of it. That means anticipating potential changes, such as when and how automakers could bring their technology and expertise into farming, and determining the necessary actions, such as forming partnerships and making equity investments. Furthermore, backcasting should delineate multiple futures with different breakpoints and timings based on possible combinations of analog and digital technologies. The seamless integration of silicon and steel will co-occur differently across all industries. Therefore, exploring alternative future trajectories by benchmarking adjacent areas equips incumbents to effectively manage their ability to defend current profits while going after new pockets of value.

Principle Two: Design for Collaborative Intelligence

Though the organizational structure of a fusion business remains in flux, one underlying design principle is becoming clear. It's futile to treat human intelligence as separate from its machine counterpart; looking at these two resources independently is ineffective. Every function and activity will be augmented by humans and machines working together, expressed in two simple words: collaborative intelligence. Companies should shift their mindset from thinking of AI as *artificial* intelligence to thinking of it as *augmented* intelligence.

By now, it's well understood that even the smartest humans will not be as effective without powerful digital tools as they could be with them. Every competitive battle will require winners to marshal the best weapons that reflect this collaborative intelligence. Humans and machines will collaborate to cocreate advanced datagraphs and digital twins to identify patterns that were previously undetectable. The algorithms will find strong patterns to unlock value in unique situations that may be challenging for humans to analyze.

Organizational designers will increasingly delegate computationally intensive tasks to machines, focusing their own attention on decision-making processes that machines cannot yet handle.[7] When asked to rank the three essential resources for successful digital transformation—finance, technology, and human—industrial leaders consistently prioritize human resources. Industrials must reskill their talent and strategically position themselves to attract new talent. To facilitate this transition, two essential practices must be employed.

Retrain today's workforce

One of the most challenging tasks is articulating the scale, scope, and transition speed from the familiar stage where humans and machines operate independently. Most workers in industrial companies, even those with technical degrees, are not well versed in how advanced algorithms could help them perform their jobs more effectively. At the same time, every technical discipline is being reinvented with data and AI—and especially Gen AI. Even people who finished their schooling recently will find their expertise becoming obsolete. Companies like Deere have long recognized the importance of technical training; it started a tech training program in 1989. Every company must now expand to educate and train its broader workforce on the collaborative nature of humans and machines.

Our discussions with companies have revealed their increased attention to training specialists in cybersecurity, blockchain, cloud computing, advanced AI, and other digital technologies. That's a good start, but what's needed is a more comprehensive understanding of where and how human and machine intelligence intersects across the board and what needs to be done to be productive now. We advocate for more general training on how Gen AI algorithms complement human skills.

Building tripartite digital twins with data in motion, collected and analyzed in real time, is a new challenge. But this task needs to be understood by a broad cross-section of managers. Designing databases with graph structures that use predictive analytics to develop customized solutions is a new task. Some workers might excel in the technical details, but everyone should be proficient in using such databases to derive insights. Not everyone may be technically savvy in Gen AI, but everyone should be proficient in using the available tools to be more productive. Knitting together products and equipment from different competitors across distinct domains, and making the data flow seamlessly in complex systems, is becoming a new critical competence.

Running industrial operations centers with the same speed and efficiency as modern tech operations, like those of Google and Amazon, requires new discipline. Humans can do this and more only by partnering with machines; at the same time, machines need human input and involvement. Industrials should elevate these partnerships to be a top priority since there's so much confusion about when and how technology could cause significant unemployment. Investments in training the workforce on collaborative intelligence will have an immediate and considerable payoff.

Recruit tomorrow's talent base

The emphasis on how humans and machines collaborate to accelerate collaborative intelligence will evolve. Therefore, training today's workforce is a start but not the end. The talent base will change as industries become digital, and it will change as the choice of where and how to compete shifts.

At its annual AI Day, Tesla showcases its unique offerings by unveiling technological advancements like proprietary chips and presenting the digital teams assembled to drive innovation. The real audience of AI Day, though, is not industry observers or financial analysts—it's future employees. If you ask Mercedes-Benz, Volkswagen, Ford, and GM about their talent priorities, their answers would be about hiring top-tier software engineers and AI experts who may not have given much thought to working in industrial companies. Industrials must strive to recruit those who see their role as collaborating with machines, continually learning, and being early evangelists.

If Deere turns out to be the talk of the town on its 200th anniversary, we would expect the company to have a different talent base than it did when the smart industrial strategy was announced in 2020. It would have a strong cadre of specialist data scientists that fine-tune their proprietary algorithms to make farming productive and sustainable. But more would be needed. Deere would have recruited talent that can seamlessly combine its expertise with digital technologies at the top tier of professional competence. And the disciplinary experts would be comfortable and willing to work with data scientists to unlock business value. Thus Deere's talent base would match its aspirations as the company continues to evolve beyond a historical focus on machines and becomes a trusted solutions provider for its customers.

Progressively, Deere would have extended the logic of collaborative intelligence beyond its corporate boundaries and into critical partners in its ecosystem. As digital technologies grow more powerful and autonomous, they will be integrated across various functions and involve suppliers, dealers, distributors, and partners. Leaders must leverage the technology stack's evolution to unlock value, proactively balancing decision rights and authority between humans and machines and ensuring critical partners keep pace. As Gen AI technologies become more prevalent in different industries, leaders must continually push the frontier of what should be delegated to algorithms and what should be done collaboratively.

Winners will be defined by their ability to have the entire organization, including its extended ecosystems, recognize and respond to collaborative intelligence's power and fast-evolving dynamics. And they will have balanced the velocities of retraining and recruitment.

Principle Three: Live (and Grow) in Ecosystems

Beyond collaborative intelligence between humans and machines, another form of cooperation takes center stage as competitive battles shift from using smart machines to solving customer problems. The networks of relationships between companies across industries erase traditional boundaries. Success will depend on creating alliances, partnerships, ecosystems, and consortiums; cooperating with allies; and forming new patterns of digital business relationships. Winners will be "we companies" rather than "me companies," with competitive advantage arising from their positions within the overlapping ecosystems they create or join.

This is a significant shift for historically monolithic industries with proprietary technologies, which have preferred clear demarcation between competition and cooperation. The digital world demands that they compete and interconnect through ecosystems, working closely with customers and earning their trust. This requires getting privileged access to customer data, embedding deep in client operations, and building the trust needed to prescribe actions that impact customer profitability. Two practices are essential for achieving this new dynamic.

Make ecosystems deliver today

A company's revenue and profits depend on how well it leverages its partners to complement its internal competencies. For Deere, this would involve ensuring that its portfolio of partners, including its channel partners, technology partners, and those involved in precision agriculture—including some of its likely future competitors, such as Monsanto and AGCO—are structured to maximize profits. In addition, it would need to explore the role of partners for sensors, software, satellite imagery, and field mapping, as well as specialists in dealing with data interoperability. These are unfamiliar partners whose competencies will be required to help Deere accelerate its transformation from a maker of analog machines and equipment to a leader that has comprehensively utilized tripartite twins to digitize its entire product life cycle, with data in motion fed into datagraphs to reveal ways to continually improve product performance.

The portfolio of partnerships in this first stage of transition is a solid foundation as Deere delineates responsibilities to manage the different relationships in a coordinated manner. Historically, some relationships would have been addressed by the purchasing function, with its standard protocols and rules, while others may be within the marketing and service function, with its own performance metrics and oversight procedures. Our strategy playbook calls for these relationships to be structured and managed in a coordinated manner so that data from the machines in the field flows to the different partners as needed. Deere could succeed not by relying only on its internal competencies, but by streamlining the coordination with its portfolio of partners. And the portfolio is managed not just to design and deliver the machines, but to monitor how they perform in the field over their life cycles. This new guiding principle should help Deere adopt a coordinated partnership approach rather than treating the different partnerships as independent business arrangements.

Adapt your ecosystems for tomorrow

Our strategy framework is dynamic, implying that the portfolio of relationships will and must change, and that's the focus of this practice. Deere must develop new relationships with soil, seed, fertilizer, chemical, water, weather, and insurance companies to effectively step up to fusion solutions. As the company explores new trajectories on the fusion strategy matrix, it must assess which new competencies to internalize (through acquisitions or internal developments) and which to access through partnerships. Fusion frontiers and emerging competitive battles transform the portfolio of competencies that an industrial has developed over time. They turn critical relationships into hygiene factors, necessitate new capabilities as technologies gain commercial viability, and provide future protection against unknown competitors with novel, unproven technologies.

Our playbook suggests that leaders look at ecosystems to understand possible trajectories and the timing of shifting from one battleground to another (for example, from brilliant machines to the showdown of smart systems). What partnerships could help Deere become a leader with precision farming systems beyond its portfolio of machines? What capabilities must be optimized before Deere shifts its strategy? Where could it push further with its collaborations with Microsoft cloud functionality and Gen AI to enhance its ontology of how the complex interrelationships in precision agriculture could be leveraged to deliver customized solutions? What could it do to enhance its partnership with Amazon Web Services to evolve the functionality of its operations center? Should Deere take a minority equity investment in satellite companies to ensure that its millions of machines (plus those of its partners) steadily transmit data back to the operations center, while also taking advantage of satellite connectivity to remotely fine-tune the machines in the field?[8]

Due to digital technologies' ever-changing opportunities and challenges, companies must continually rebalance their relationships and ecosystems. It's crucial to proactively assess key trends and react swiftly to market moves as competitors restructure their partnerships and ecosystems to gain an advantage.

Backcasting can aid in determining how relationships should be rebalanced within an ecosystem. For example, if electric drive trains from trucks could be adapted for agriculture and construction machines in a modular architecture, how could they shift the competitive landscape and cost structures? Should Deere experiment to understand the benefits and challenges instead of waiting for a prototype to be shown at a trade show? Addressing these kinds of questions can help companies proactively adapt their ecosystems.

Principle Four: Nurture Fusion Leaders

Fusion leaders combine the best attributes of traditional and digital-native organizations. Industrial digital transformation is unlike anything that has preceded it in the past few decades. Our logic of four battlefields, and the corresponding winning strategies in each, requires leaders to see this moment as calling not for incremental adjustments but for fundamental reinventions.

In our research, we have identified key leadership characteristics. Individuals who possess these qualities acknowledge their company's technological and managerial legacies while recognizing that past success does not guarantee a prosperous future. They challenge deeply ingrained biases and embrace digital technology to transform every aspect of the business. They may not be deep technical experts, but they comprehend the impact and power of digital technologies in shifting the competitive landscape and rewriting the rules of value creation and capture. They intuitively understand the power of data and of insights from data that can be gleaned through powerful algorithms. They are open to data-driven ideas that may challenge their received wisdom and past routines. They are systems thinkers who skillfully connect the dots to articulate a future vision and effectively communicate its opportunities and challenges. The question, then, is how to develop and nurture such leaders. Two practices must be deployed.

Cultivate fusion thinking within the C-suite

Unsurprisingly, fusion leadership starts at the top. But most top management teams in industrial companies have differing views regarding digitization's scale, scope, and speed. This misalignment directly results in the misallocation of scarce resources. Too often, the team overallocates resources to routine activities and historical competencies, and underallocates resources to initiatives likely to define the future. There's a tendency at first to believe that digital technologies will affect only some parts of the business and thus aren't a top priority. So, some teams are content to delegate the deployment of fusion strategies to the IT function or, at best, create ad hoc teams. What we have found most important is a shared view of how, when, and where digital drives strategy and shifts the competitive battles. That unified view helps ensure a common list of strategic priorities and associated resource allocations across the time horizons discussed earlier.

Fusion leaders ensure that every function understands digitization's transformative power and the trade-offs that must be made across functions to design the new foundations for the future. John May did this at Deere to ensure that the smart industrial strategy is not just a marketing slogan and that the entire C-suite was fully committed to the new vision. And by hiring the Boston Consulting Group partner who helped articulate this strategy to be the new president of life cycle solutions, supply management, and customer success, May communicated the need for and importance of bringing in outside leaders who thread the proverbial needle between business and digital domains.

Inculcate fusion thinking throughout the organization

Establishing a unified view of fusion futures within the C-suite is an excellent beginning, but success ultimately relies on everyone's embracing the direction and pace of transformation. Because digital transformation is a matter of changing business processes, mindsets, and culture, it is accomplished most efficiently when it doesn't simply trickle down from the top. The more that managers learn to use the principles of fusion strategies, the more likely it is that change will happen faster, with less friction and confusion.

Consequently, it is urgent to reskill internal talent across all levels and functions, preparing them for the fusion future. The early warning signs are when the historical gulf between traditional disciplines and digital technologies continues to operate. To overcome this, educate and upskill employees at the intersection of their traditional domain skills and digital technology. Enable them to work with technologies that automate their current jobs, allowing their expertise to be applied where machines may not be as effective today. Implement hackathons and other innovation initiatives to inform everyone of potential technology shifts. Additionally, position the organization in the talent marketplace as being at the forefront of technology adoption, creating a positive perception among potential employees.

Principle Five: Follow Your
Strategy Scorecard

Fusion shifts the competitive landscape, prompting companies to transition from products to services, systems, and solutions. In the absence of a strategy scorecard with specific metrics and timeframes, there is a high probability that transformational efforts will fail. We caution companies against using generic scorecards (or unthinkingly following someone else's) and highlight the importance of developing a scorecard that reflects the company's aspirations, reference points, resources, and target milestones.

It's essential to consider what the company excludes as much as what it includes. Should the metrics focus more on defending the core business than on pursuing new opportunities? Does the scorecard consider how digital technology impacts products, processes, and services and their potential obsolescence? Are there metrics that track the most desirable customers for services and solutions? Has the company focused enough on identifying current and future partners that can contribute to immediate profits and long-term success in various fusion scenarios? Two practices must be instituted.

Use metrics that match the battles

Companies often use vague goals like "We aspire to be the market leader" or "We want to be number one." However, scorecards should be precise, ensuring everyone knows the criteria, achievements, and gaps. When engaging in the four strategy battles, companies must provide the entire organization with an understanding of the short- and long-term success metrics. Too often, leaders communicate the "what" of metrics without the "why." Implementation will be ineffective without clearly articulating the what and the why. For Deere, this means that the metrics should be focused not on the number of machines sold or the after-market profitability from services, but on the impact on customer productivity and profitability at the level of a portfolio of crops and on the long-term sustainable use of scarce resources.

Privacy and security are particularly relevant metrics as industrial machines interconnect across boundaries. Industrials must earn customers' and partners' trust by safeguarding their data and demonstrating a commitment to data security. The privacy and security of industrial data can provide a competitive edge; continually track failures and showcase the metrics to gain customer trust.

Quantification has limits, and it can't identify surprise shifts. Fusion scorecards should allow stakeholders to bring up outliers or weak signals, indicating discontinuities. Digital innovations often emerge at these intersections, and early identification can help the industrials seize the first-mover advantage.

Shift when the metrics do

Using fusion as a strategy lens helps industrials think about their evolution from providers of fusion products to providers of fusion solutions as the strategy battles evolve. These shifts must be planned and executed based on metrics. Companies must ensure that scorecards track parameters that indicate when the current strategy is under stress because markets or rivals have changed, and when other fusion strategies have become possible and profitable. As Deere shifts its approach to becoming a solutions company, for example, the metrics should also change, emphasizing customers' perceptions of Deere as a trusted strategic partner rather than the number of machines operating in different locations.

. . .

Deere is already well on its way with fusion services, with a technology stack that has evolved steadily over the last twenty-five years. It's by no means a latecomer to the digital industrial transformation, although May's actions in recent years have given more clarity to the company's future aspirations. The company's investor presentation in 2022 showed the evolution in the tech stack along five distinct layers: hardware and software, guidance, connectivity and digital solutions, automation, and autonomy. If we were to reflect on the fundamental principles of fusion strategy and extrapolate a tech stack, we would add datagraphs and AI to fuel the shift from smart machines (Deere's current distinctive position in the market) to fusion solutions (its stated ambition). These two layers, added at appropriate times in the coming years, would help Deere become the talk of the town in 2037. Our argument is simple and applies to every industrial company: to think beyond making its machines operate autonomously and to build a network of machines that transmit data to be fed into powerful AI algorithms to derive contextually relevant prescriptions that unlock significant value that remains trapped today.

Fusion Forward

CEOs of asset-heavy industrial companies must realize that now is the time to seize the opportunities presented by the battlegrounds of digital transformation: the battle of brilliant machines, the race to deliver remarkable results, the showdown of smart systems, and the clash of custom solutions. These battlegrounds will shift over time in different sectors, but they all offer opportunities for industrials to capture a fair share of the value. Business leaders must develop the capability to recognize the signals that indicate the relative attractiveness of the different battlegrounds, make sense of competitive moves and technology developments, and take decisive actions to secure a competitive edge in the ever-evolving fusion landscape.

In the battle of brilliant machines, recognize that digital-first architecture will eventually win. Ensure that your road map takes this into account as you adjust your investments in the fusion of advanced technologies to elevate your products' performance and capabilities.

In the race to deliver remarkable results, focus on embedding your organization deeply into customer operations, leveraging data and analytics to drive service excellence and customer profitability. In doing so, you become irreplaceable by the alternatives that lack deep expertise.

Navigate the showdown of smart systems by determining your role in interconnected ecosystems and being agile in architecting and managing dataflows within these systems. You must also adapt your company's role as the shapes of systems change.

Finally, in the clash of custom solutions, equip your organization with the power of Gen AI and deep domain knowledge to create tailored offerings that address customer needs in real time.

The time has come to be decisive. Data and AI are not tomorrow's opportunities; they are today's challenges. In our conversations with

CEOs of industrial companies, one common thread emerges: They know that digital will undoubtedly disrupt and reorder the competitive landscape. They recognize that they must become digital-first with more attention to data and AI. That's no longer questioned in boardrooms. The only disagreements are around the timing and the speed of resource reallocations: how fast to let go of yesterday's competencies and build new ones for tomorrow, how quickly to let go of the relationships that may not be as critical for the future, and how rapidly to conduct a makeover of the talent portfolio.

CEOs must address and resolve those issues immediately. Table 9-1 summarizes how Strategy *Next* (the fusion approach) is distinctly different from Strategy *Now* (the traditional approach). The fusion

TABLE 9-1

How Strategy *Now* differs from Strategy *Next*

Category	Strategy *Now* (traditional strategy)	Strategy *Next* (fusion strategy)
Growth dynamics	Linear, gradual, within industry boundaries	Nonlinear, exponential, across industry boundaries
Competitive landscape	Familiar competitors with similar business models focused on products as designed and delivered	Digital natives as competitors with new capabilities focused on products as used
Scale and efficiency	Physical assets; production-based scale	Information assets; data-based scale
Scope expansion	Product-market extensions; vertical integration through mergers and acquisitions	Competencies from datagraphs; virtual integration through data integration and partnerships
Customer insights	Ad hoc surveys; operational improvement; insights limited to the points of purchase	Real-time observations; competitive differentiation; insights on links to customer outcomes
Network effects	Direct and indirect network effects	Data network effects
Data and AI strategy	Enhanced efficiency, independent databases, systems of records, engagements; firm-centric; focused on a single firm; AI for operational effectiveness	Real-time insights, integrated databases, systems of datagraphs; network-centric; focused on firms and their ecosystems of partners and customers; AI for strategic differentiation

future is not a linear extrapolation of the industrial past. Today's core competencies will not be enough to win tomorrow.

Successful companies fade away because they overinvest in what they are good at today and underinvest in what they need to be good at tomorrow. The fusion future brings that challenge front and center and compels you to act. Take inspiration from words attributed to Leonardo da Vinci: "I have been impressed with the urgency of doing. Knowing is not enough; we must apply. Being willing is not enough; we must do."

A Note on Scholarly Foundations and a Call for Action

OUR COLLABORATION IS ITSELF AN EXAMPLE OF FUSION: VG's interests in strategy and innovation infused with Venkat's long-standing quest to turn digital into a prime driver of value creation. Those seemingly disparate interests come together in this book.

Historically, the academic fields of strategy and information technology have operated in silos. Strategy scholars—guided by economic models and behavioral research—treated information systems and technologies as functional-level tactics that were meant merely to respond to higher-level choices of corporate scope (what's in the company's portfolio) and business strategy (how to compete in each chosen business).

In the 1980s, a group of scholars at Harvard and MIT recognized the power of information technologies. Venkat was fortunate to start his career in strategy at the MIT Sloan School of Management. He was invited to participate in a forward-focused research program in the mid-1980s that had an overarching question: How can businesses transform themselves by taking advantage of the power of information technology, and what could it mean for the discipline of management as we know it?[1]

At that time, Digital Equipment Corporation was beginning to challenge IBM's superiority in mainframes with minicomputers. Still, those were early days for information technology. The most potent piece of hardware for professionals was an IBM personal computer, and the most versatile software program (a "killer application") was Lotus 1-2-3 from a startup in Cambridge, Massachusetts. Michael Porter's 1985 *Harvard Business Review* article, "How Information Gives You Competitive Advantage," was prescient long before the current focus on data and AI.[2] At that time, Silicon Valley was in a distant orbit. Tim Berners-Lee at CERN would pen his famous memo about architecting the web in 1989.[3]

It all began to change in the 1990s. There were calls to redesign business processes and reengineer corporations by taking advantage of the power of enterprise systems from Oracle, SAP, and Microsoft. Sure, such systems needed significant resources in terms of money, people, and management time. However, the focus was to make companies more efficient in their chosen strategy, not change the way they build competitive advantage. Strategy—regarding where and how to compete—continued to march to the traditional tunes. The gulf between the academic disciplines remained, even as a 1993 article published by Venkat and a colleague in *IBM Systems Journal* was heralded in 1999 as a turning point in thinking about the much-needed alignment between business and IT.[4]

The introduction of the web browser, the rapid growth of the internet, and the emergence of dot-com startups changed the perception and understanding of the power of digital technologies. Scholars began to notice and started to talk about how new entrants could challenge incumbents through data (Google in advertising), disintermediation (Amazon in retailing), and disruption (Netflix in media). These were not efficiency moves but transformative entrepreneurial ideas that leveraged the power of digital technologies. Marketing scholars began to theorize the role of market spaces and the power of long tail as new concepts for gaining advantage. At the height of the dot-com boom, Venkat wrote an article in *MIT Sloan Management Review* on how incumbents should exploit the internet to both defend core activities and design new ones—a central theme echoed by VG in framing the three-box solution for strategic innovation.[5]

As the web grew and matured, and with Apple's introduction of the iPhone in 2007 and Google's follow-up with the Android operating system, the possibilities of new business models mushroomed. Economics and strategy scholars conceptualized the potential power of multisided platforms to disrupt the status quo.[6] Amazon, YouTube, Uber, Airbnb, Facebook, Instagram, and others demonstrated new business models that introduced new ways to create and capture value. Theories and empirical work showed how such models operate in multisided markets, often subsidizing one side with another, leveraging network effects, and creating scale without ownership, while involving diverse types of partners and taking advantage of the power of rapid feedback effects. Over the past decade, scholars from different subfields in business have finally found a common ground in understanding the role and benefits of platform business models, including ecosystems and the role of complementors.[7]

Digital platforms operate primarily in asset-light settings but could threaten asset-heavy sectors by shifting value from traditional artifacts (namely products) to newer offerings (for example, services wrapped around products), as in the case of Uber or Airbnb. In addition, scholars realized that many industrial settings could be easily disrupted and transformed by digital technologies without the need for platform business models. The field of information systems recognized the emergence of digital business strategy as an essential theme in 2013, when the editors of *MIS Quarterly* proclaimed that the time had come to consider a fusion between IT strategy and business strategy.[8] They argued that the impact of digital is cross-functional, that digital should be seen not as piecemeal technologies such as the web or databases or enterprise systems but as organizational resources (consistent with the resource-based view of the firm, familiar to strategy scholars), and that digital technologies impact business performance beyond efficiency improvements. The hoped-for fusion between the two academic fields, however, failed to materialize. Nonetheless, books and articles aimed at practitioners and based on the fusion idea proliferated, calling on strategists to recognize the transformative power of digital technologies.[9]

VG saw firsthand how digital technologies could reshape industrial companies when he was GE's first professor in residence and chief innovation consultant during 2008 and 2009. At that time, GE was in the early stages of exploring ways to leverage the industrial internet to create customer value.[10]

The third decade of the twenty-first century is here. In this digital decade, we are seeing digital technologies impact every industry and every company in every geography. The leaderboard of highly capitalized companies already consists of Apple, Microsoft, Alphabet, Amazon, Meta, Nvidia, and Tesla. With generative AI (Gen AI), they are reinventing themselves and challenging companies that may be unable to assimilate new technologies. These companies are the rule makers as every industry digitizes rapidly.

Unfortunately, many business schools continue to house digital and strategy faculty in different departments, artificially separated with little cross-functional collaboration in research. Perhaps it also reflects the separation of premier scholarly journals in each field. Continuing to research how corporations should operate and how managers should lead is unacceptable without a coherent body of research foundations that recognize the extent to which digital permeates every facet of our lives.

Studying product innovations only through the lens of engineering and technology management, without recognizing the power of computing and algorithms, is myopic. Nearly every product is now a digital product or interfaces with one, and their architectures likely resemble a tech stack more than analog versions. It's insufficient to examine the delivery of customer service value through marketing scholarship without considering how much it relies on digital through elegant models and mathematical proofs. One fruitful avenue would be to describe and analyze carefully crafted case studies of next-practice companies and their transformation from analog to digital—similar to the research methods of Argyris, Lawrence, Porter, and others we've highlighted.

VG was fortunate to meet Elon Musk in 2016 when the innovator described his vision of designing a car that would be a computer on wheels and connected to the cloud. Going from internal combustion engines to electric vehicles to self-driving cars is a paradigm shift. VG's initial exposure to GE and subsequent encounter with Musk convinced him that the laws of competitive advantage have changed, rewarding those who have the most robust real-time insights rather than the most valuable physical assets. Our in-depth field studies in over a dozen industrial companies reinforced the notion that the fusion future is not a linear extrapolation of the industrial past. Fusion signifies fundamental shifts. The competitive landscape changes, the competencies required are different, new ecosystems emerge, and the process of value creation transforms. Refer back to table 9-1, which summarizes how fusion strategy distinctly differs from traditional strategy.

We are in the beginning stages of the digitization of the industrial sector, hence it is a fertile ground for future research. Gen AI, the next inflection point in the evolution of AI, will put fusion strategy on steroids. With the technology able to, among other things, generate complex designs, extract insights and trends from multimodal data, predict and respond proactively to changing conditions, and handle ambiguous and incomplete data, Gen AI is tailor-made to transform the logic of competition in industrial businesses. The emerging business landscape—the fusion future in front of industrial companies—invites scholars to develop novel approaches that could lead to next-generation strategy insights.

As we worked on this book's manuscript, we revisited the question that guided the scholars in the mid-1980s. We repeat that question here with a small but important word change:

architecture and how far-reaching its implications are on oth
organizational functions and potentially on extended business ec
systems. It's inadequate to research supply chain configuration
without considering how the internet of things and Industry 4.0 driv
supply chain innovations and signal broader shifts in global corporations' geographic loci. It's short-sighted to think that data and AI
will impact only "high-tech sectors" when Gen AI will likely affect a
large swath of the global economy in the coming decade.[11] Financial
analysis for strategic decisions will be misleading and might even be
downright wrong if scholars do not account for intangible assets, the
principal resources of the digital era. Organizational learning should
be reconceptualized as human intelligence augmented by machine
learning. Strategies that companies have traditionally employed to
manage information technologies for efficiency may not be equally effective when navigating generative AI systems focused on creativity.

The field of strategy that is the intellectual home to both of us has
been built on detailed field studies carried out by scholars with different disciplinary orientations: Ken Andrews with a general management
heritage; Alfred Chandler with a business history approach; Chris Argyris from an organizational learning standpoint; Michael Porter
from an economic viewpoint; Paul Lawrence and Jay Lorsch with an
organizational theory method; C.K. Prahalad with a resources and
competencies lens; Clay Christensen from a disruptive innovation
view, and so on. These scholars conducted multiyear case studies on
legendary companies such as GM, GE, IBM, Westinghouse, Kodak,
Hewlett-Packard, Honda, Sony, and Caterpillar. Generations of students have been schooled on the ideas of these academic luminaries.

We are now in an era when a new set of born-digital companies
are writing new strategy rules, and industrial companies are rapidly
evolving to adapt and reinvent themselves. This historical moment
calls for innovations in how strategy research is conducted. Such innovations, we hope, will be liberated from the old shackles of theories,
models, and assumptions, informed by—but certainly not constrained
by—narrowly defined theories or the need to offer universal truths

How can businesses transform themselves by taking advantage of the power of *digital* technology, and what could it mean for the discipline of management as we know it?

There is no longer any doubt that digital technologies will impact companies; the only unknown is how extensive (scale and scope) and how fast (speed) that process will be. It is also becoming apparent that digital—especially data and AI—will impact the discipline of management just as it has begun to impact different branches of physical sciences, social sciences, and engineering.

While working with companies, we have called upon them to innovate and reinvent. We would be remiss if we did not call upon the academic profession to do the same—especially now, when we know that many ideas must be reexamined and that several should be selectively forgotten (in the spirit of the three-box solution). Theories and research findings that were conceptualized and tested with data in the industrial age should be reconceptualized and tested with data from companies as they strive to adapt to the fusion future. It is time to fuse the two academic fields—strategy and digital—together into an inseparable whole.

NOTES

Chapter 1

1. Alfred Chandler Jr.'s classic book, *Scale and Scope: The Dynamics of Industrial Capitalism,* still underpins strategic thinking in academic and practitioner circles.

2. We use the word "digitals" to refer to companies that were born digital in the late twentieth and early twenty-first century; these organizations do not have the legacy constraints of the industrials that grew up in the mid- to late twentieth century. We use the terms "industrials" (as parallel to the digitals) and "industrial companies" interchangeably.

3. McKinsey and Company, "What Is the Metaverse?," McKinsey, August 17, 2022, https://www.mckinsey.com/featured-insights/mckinsey-explainers/what-is-the-metaverse. Although McKinsey estimates that by 2030, the metaverse could add $5 trillion, or a 2 to 3 percent increase, to the expected gross domestic product, we believe that the lower bound is 1 percent, based on realistic shifts in the industrial sectors.

4. Mark Harris, "Tesla's Autopilot Depends on a Deluge of Data," IEEE Spectrum, August 4, 2022, https://spectrum.ieee.org/tesla-autopilot-data-deluge.

5. We build from our *Harvard Business Review* article "The Next Great Digital Advantage" (May–June 2022), which introduced our ideas on datagraphs.

6. Don Reisinger, "All Companies Should Live by the Jeff Bezos 70 Percent Rule," Inc., June 27, 2020, https://www.inc.com/don-reisinger/all-companies-should-live-by-jeff-bezos-70-percent-rule.html.

Chapter 2

1. Bill Ready, "Working with Merchants to Give You More Ways to Shop," The Keyword, May 18, 2021, https://blog.google/products/shopping/more-ways-to-shop.

2. For an updated overview of Google's Shopping Graph, see Randy Rockinson, "4 Ways Google's Shopping Graph Helps You Find What You Want," The Keyword, February 7, 2023, https://blog.google/products/shopping/shopping-graph-explained.

3. "Data Is the New Gold. This Is How It Can Benefit Everyone—While Harming No One," World Economic Forum, July 29, 2020, https://www.weforum.org

/agenda/2020/07/new-paradigm-business-data-digital-economy-benefits-privacy
-digitalization.

4. For a general overview, see Albert-László Barabási's book *Linked: The New
Science of Networks* (New York: Basic Books, 2014); Sangeet Paul Choudary, "The
Rise of Social Graphs for Businesses," hbr.org, February 2, 2015, https://hbr.org
/2015/02/the-rise-of-social-graphs-for-businesses.

5. "From Discovery to Checkout: Shopify and Google Deepen Commerce Collaboration," Shopify, May 27, 2021, https://news.shopify.com/from-discovery-to
-checkout-shopify-and-google-deepen-commerce-collaboration.

6. "Satya Nadella Email to LinkedIn Employees on Acquisition," Microsoft
News Center, June 13, 2016, https://news.microsoft.com/2016/06/13/satya-nadella
-email-to-linkedin-employees-on-acquisition/.

7. For those interested in more details on Microsoft Graph, see "Overview of
Microsoft Graph," Microsoft, March 15, 2023, https://learn.microsoft.com/en-us
/graph/overview.

8. Amit Singhal, "Introducing the Knowledge Graph: Things, Not Strings,"
The Keyword, May 16, 2012, https://blog.google/products/search/introducing
-knowledge-graph-things-not.

9. "WPP Partners with Nvidia to Build Generative AI-Enabled Content Engine for Digital Advertising," Nvidia Newsroom, May 28, 2023, https://nvidianews
.nvidia.com/news/wpp-partners-with-nvidia-to-build-generative-ai-enabled
-content-engine-for-digital-advertising.

Chapter 3

1. For an overview of Industry 4.0, see "Fourth Industrial Revolution," World
Economic Forum, accessed October 17, 2023, https://www.weforum.org/focus
/fourth-industrial-revolution.

2. "Our Leadership Team: John C. May," John Deere, accessed October 16,
2023, https://www.deere.com/en/our-company/leadership/may-john-c/.

3. For more on Volkswagen's New Auto strategy, see "Volkswagen Focuses Development for Autonomous Driving," Volkswagen Group News, October 26, 2022,
https://www.volkswagen-newsroom.com/en/press-releases/volkswagen-focuses
-development-for-autonomous-driving-15271.

4. See, for example, "The Economic Potential of Generative AI: The Next Productivity Frontier," McKinsey Digital, June 14, 2023, https://www.mckinsey.com
/capabilities/mckinsey-digital/our-insights/the-economic-potential-of-generative
-ai-the-next-productivity-frontier#business-value.

5. To read Bloomberg's announcement, see "Introducing BloombergGPT,
Bloomberg's 50-Billion Parameter Large Language Model, Purpose-Built from
Scratch for Finance," Bloomberg, March 30, 2023, https://www.bloomberg.com
/company/press/bloomberggpt-50-billion-parameter-llm-tuned-finance. For those
interested in the detailed academic article, see https://arxiv.org/abs/2303.17564.

6. Sal Khan, "Harnessing GPT-4 So That All Students Benefit. A Nonprofit
Approach for Equal Access," Khan Academy, March 14, 2023, https://blog

.khanacademy.org/harnessing-ai-so-that-all-students-benefit-a-nonprofit
-approach-for-equal-access.

7. For an overview of R² Data Labs, visit "Digital-First Culture," Rolls-Royce, accessed October 17, 2023, https://www.rolls-royce.com/innovation/digital/r2-data-labs.aspx.

8. For those interested in details of how Netflix builds its ontology as a key part of its recommender system, visit "Recommendations: Figuring Out How to Bring Unique Joy to Each Member," Netflix Research, accessed October 17, 2023, https://research.netflix.com/research-area/recommendations.

9. For more on how Airbnb develops its knowledge graph, see Xiaoya Wei, "Contextualizing Airbnb by Building Knowledge Graph," Medium, January 29, 2019, https://medium.com/airbnb-engineering/contextualizing-airbnb-by-building-knowledge-graph-b7077e268d5a.

10. For more details on how Uber uses datagraphs to improve its operations and deliver differentiated services, see Ankit Jain et al., "Food Discovery with Uber Eats: Using Graph Learning to Power Recommendations," Uber Blog, December 4, 2019, https://www.uber.com/blog/uber-eats-graph-learning.

11. For use cases on industrial knowledge graphs at Siemens, see Thomas Hubauer, "Use Cases of the Industrial Knowledge Graph at Siemens," *International Workshop on the Semantic Web* (2018), https://ceur-ws.org/Vol-2180/paper-86.pdf; for an overview of knowledge graphs at Bosch, see Sebastian Monka et al., "Learning Visual Models Using a Knowledge Graph as a Trainer," Bosch Research Blog, July 28, 2022, https://www.bosch.com/stories/knowledge-driven-machine-learning; for more on how Rolls-Royce taps into knowledge graphs and AI, see "Tapping AI Technologies to Create Solutions of Tomorrow," Rolls-Royce, accessed October 17, 2023, https://www.rolls-royce.com/country-sites/sea/discover/2021/tapping-ai-technologies-to-create-solutions-of-tomorrow.aspx.

12. For more details on areas of application, see, for instance, "Generative AI," BCG, accessed October 17, 2023, https://www.bcg.com/capabilities/artificial-intelligence/generative-ai.

13. Elliott Grant, "Machine Learning Is Imperfect. That's Why It's Ideal for Agriculture," Mineral, April 27, 2023, https://mineral.ai/blog/machine-learning-is-imperfect-thats-why-its-ideal-for-agriculture.

Chapter 4

1. Michael Porter's three generic strategies have been the dominant strategy framework since the 1980s.

2. "Data, Insights and Action," Rolls-Royce, https://www.rolls-royce.com/country-sites/india/discover/2018/data-insight-action-latest.aspx.

3. "GE Aviation: Soaring Apart from Competition with Data Analytics," Harvard Business School Digital Initiative, Technology and Operations Management, MBA Student Perspectives, November 15, 2017, https://d3.harvard.edu/platform-rctom/submission/ge-aviation-soaring-apart-from-competition-with-data-analytics.

4. "Introducing Yocova," Rolls-Royce, February 10, 2020, https://www.rolls-royce.com/media/press-releases/2020/10-02-2020-intelligentengine-introducing-yocova-a-new-digital-platform-designed.aspx.

5. Marc Andreessen, "Why Software Is Eating the World," Andreessen Horowitz, August 20, 2011, https://a16z.com/2011/08/20/why-software-is-eating-the-world.

6. Marc Andreessen, "It's Time to Build," Andreessen Horowitz, April 18, 2020, https://a16z.com/2020/04/18/its-time-to-build.

Chapter 5

1. "Master Plan Part 3," Tesla, April 5, 2023, https://www.tesla.com/ns_videos/Tesla-Master-Plan-Part-3.pdf

2. Brandon Bernicky, Twitter post, November 12, 2019, https://twitter.com/brandonbernicky/status/1194444012494761989.

3. For background on how Waymo built it, see Dmitri Dolgov, "How We've Built the World's Most Experienced Urban Driver," Waymo, August 19, 2021, https://waymo.com/blog/2021/08/MostExperiencedUrbanDriver.html.

4. "Mercedes-Benz and Nvidia: Software-Defined Computing Architecture for Automated Driving Across Future Fleet," Mercedes-Benz Group, June 23, 2020, https://group.mercedes-benz.com/innovation/product-innovation/autonomous-driving/mercedes-benz-and-nvidia-plan-cooperation.html.

5. Angus MacKenzie, "Mercedes-Benz CEO Ola Källenius on EVs Reinventing the Three-Pointed Star," *MotorTrend*, July 26, 2023, https://www.motortrend.com/features/mercedes-benz-ceo-ola-kallenius-2023-ev-interview.

6. "FIAT Metaverse Store, the World's First Metaverse-Powered Showroom, a Revolution in Customer Experience," Stellantis, December 1, 2022, https://www.media.stellantis.com/em-en/fiat/press/fiat-metaverse-store-the-world-s-first-metaverse-powered-showroom-a-revolution-in-customer-experience.

7. "Toyota Research Institute Unveils New Generative AI Technique for Vehicle Design," Toyota Newsroom, June 20, 2023, https://pressroom.toyota.com/toyota-research-institute-unveils-new-generative-ai-technique-for-vehicle-design.

8. Jeff Immelt, "Digital Change Is Hard for Industrial Companies," LinkedIn, March 12, 2019, https://www.linkedin.com/pulse/digital-change-hard-industrial-companies-jeff-immelt.

9. For more details on how Tesla collects and analyzes such data, see Mark Harris, "The Radical Scope of Tesla's Data Hoard," *IEEE Spectrum*, August 3, 2022, https://spectrum.ieee.org/tesla-autopilot-data-scope.

10. This colloquial term, attributed to Ward Cunningham, was formalized in 2016 at a seminar in Germany, where it was defined by academic and industrial experts as follows: "In software-intensive systems, technical debt is a collection of design or implementation constructs that are expedient in the short term, but set up a technical context that can make future changes more costly or impossible. Technical debt presents an actual or contingent liability whose impact is limited to internal system qualities, primarily maintainability and evolvability."

11. "Toyota Blockchain Lab, Accelerating Blockchain Technology Initiatives and External Collaboration," Toyota Newsroom, March 16, 2020, https://global.toyota /en/newsroom/corporate/31827481.html.

Chapter 6

1. Lora Kolodny, "Deere Is Paying Over $300 Million for a Start-up That Makes 'See-and-Spray' Robots," CNBC, September 6, 2017, https://www.cnbc.com/2017 /09/06/deere-is-acquiring-blue-river-technology-for-305-million.html.

2. "Sustainability at John Deere," John Deere, accessed July 23, 2023, https:// www.deere.com/en/our-company/sustainability.

3. Deere & Company, "Deere to Advance Machine Learning Capabilities in Acquisition of Blue River Technology," September 6, 2017, https://www.prnewswire .com/news-releases/deere-to-advance-machine-learning-capabilities-in -acquisition-of-blue-river-technology-300514879.html.

4. Deere & Company, "Focused on Unlocking Customer Value, Deere Announces New Operating Model," June 17, 2020, https://www.prnewswire.com /news-releases/focused-on-unlocking-customer-value-deere-announces-new -operating-model-301078608.html.

5. "CNH Industrial to Acquire Raven Industries, Enhancing Precision Agriculture Capabilities and Scale," CNH Industrial Newsroom, June 21, 2021, https://media.cnhindustrial.com/EMEA/CNH-INDUSTRIAL-CORPORATE /cnh-industrial-to-acquire-raven-industries--enhancing-precision-agriculture -capabilities-and-scale/s/8cd082be-4e36-44f0-a6ea-bfe897740e79.

6. Rob Bland et al., "Trends Driving Automation on the Farm," McKinsey & Company, May 31, 2023, https://www.mckinsey.com/industries/agriculture/our -insights/trends-driving-automation-on-the-farm.

7. Brandon Webber, "Digital Agriculture: Improving Profitability," Accenture, August 28, 2020, https://www.accenture.com/us-en/insights/interactive/agriculture -solutions.

8. Shane Bryan et al., "Creating Value in Digital-Farming Solutions," McKinsey & Company, October 20, 2020, https://www.mckinsey.com/industries/agriculture /our-insights/creating-value-in-digital-farming-solutions.

9. These insights are taken from our discussions with GE executives.

10. "Intelligent Machines, Empowered People," ABB Newsroom, May 31, 2021, https://new.abb.com/news/detail/78740/intelligent-machines-empowered-people.

Chapter 7

1. Juan Pedro Tomás, "How Honeywell Helped the Burj Khalifa Become a Smart Building," RCR Wireless News, May 14, 2018, https://www.rcrwireless.com /20180514/internet-of-things/burj-khalifa-smart-building.

2. Matt Bereman et al., "Building Products in the Digital Age: It's Hard to 'Get Smart,'" McKinsey & Company, June 6, 2022, https://www.mckinsey.com

/industries/engineering-construction-and-building-materials/our-insights
/building-products-in-the-digital-age-its-hard-to-get-smart.

3. "The Last Gap in Industrial Digitization—the Deskless Worker," Honeywell Forge, accessed July 21, 2023, https://www.honeywellforge.ai/us/en/article/how -connectivity-helps-the-deskless-worker.

4. Martin Casado and Peter Lauten, "The Empty Promise of Data Moats," Andreessen Horowitz, May 9, 2019, https://a16z.com/2019/05/09/data-network -effects-moats.

5. John Hunter, "Ackoff on Systems Thinking and Management," W. Edwards Deming Institute, September 2, 2019, https://deming.org/ackoff-on-systems -thinking-and-management.

6. For more-detailed discussions of the role of orchestrators versus partici-pants in dynamic ecosystems, see chapter 6 of Venkat Venkatraman's book *The Digital Matrix: New Rules for Business Transformation through Technology* (Los Angeles: LifeTree Media, 2017).

7. See, for instance, the ideas proposed by Andreessen Horowitz in Zeya Yang and Kristina Shen, "For B2B Generative AI Apps, Is Less More?" March 30, 2023, https://a16z.com/2023/03/30/b2b-generative-ai-synthai, and Matt Bornstein and Rajko Radovanovic, "Emerging Architectures for LLM Applications," June 20, 2023, https://a16z.com/2023/06/20/emerging-architectures-for-llm-applications. We expect to see more-powerful domain-specific models to allow for fusion sys-tems to emerge in multiple settings.

8. For background on digital and regenerative agriculture, see John Foley, "How Digital Technologies Can Bring Greater Scale to Regenerative Farming," Sygenta Group, February 2021, https://www.syngentagroup.com/en/how-digital -technologies-can-bring-greater-scale-regenerative-farming. For more on the importance of ecosystems to make it work, see Tania Strauss and Pooja Chhab-ria, "What Is Regenerative Agriculture and How Can It Help Us Get to Net-Zero Food Systems. 3 Industry Leaders Explain," World Economic Forum, Decem-ber 19, 2022, https://www.weforum.org/agenda/2022/12/3-industry-leaders-on -achieving-net-zero-goals-with-regenerative-agriculture-practices.

9. "Honeywell Teams Up with Microsoft to Reshape the Industrial Workplace," Microsoft News Center, October 22, 2020, https://news.microsoft.com/2020/10 /22/honeywell-teams-up-with-microsoft-to-reshape-the-industrial-workplace; "Honeywell, SAP Launch Connected Buildings Solution to Help Operators Make Smarter Real Estate Decisions," Honeywell, May 19, 2021, https://www.honeywell .com/us/en/press/2021/05/honeywell-sap-launch-connected-buildings-solution -to-help-operators-make-smarter-real-estate-decisions.

10. The opening sentences in Tesla's announcement (see Elon Musk, "All Our Patent Are Belong to You, Tesla, June 12, 2014, https://www.tesla.com/blog/all-our -patent-are-belong-you) are powerful: "Yesterday, there was a wall of Tesla patents in the lobby of our Palo Alto headquarters. That is no longer the case. They have been removed, in the spirit of the open source movement, for the advancement of electric vehicle technology."

11. Gil Appel, Juliana Neelbauer, and David A. Schweidel, "Generative AI Has an Intellectual Property Problem," hbr.org, April 17, 2023, https://hbr.org/2023/04/generative-ai-has-an-intellectual-property-problem.

12. R. V. Guha, "Data Commons: Making Sustainability Data Accessible," The Keyword, April 21, 2022, https://blog.google/outreach-initiatives/sustainability/data-commons-sustainability.

13. See, for instance, the lessons summarized in this article: Robert L. Grossman, "Ten Lessons for Data Sharing with a Data Commons," *Scientific Data* 10, no. 120 (2023), https://www.nature.com/articles/s41597-023-02029-x.

Chapter 8

1. Shelby Myers, "Analyzing Farm Inputs: The Cost to Farms Keeps Rising," American Farm Bureau Federation, March 17, 2022, https://www.fb.org/market-intel/analyzing-farm-inputs-the-cost-to-farm-keeps-rising.

2. "The Cash-less Amazon Go Store," Vested Finance, accessed October 17, 2023, https://vestedfinance.com/in/blog/the-cashier-less-amazon-go-store/.

3. "Digital Engineering and Manufacturing," Accenture, accessed April 7, 2023, https://www.accenture.com/us-en/insights/industry-x-index.

4. "Mineral," X—the Moonshot Factory, accessed April 7, 2023, https://x.company/projects/mineral.

Chapter 9

1. "2023 Deere & Company at a Glance," John Deere, 2023, https://www.deere.com/assets/pdfs/common/our-company/deere-&-company-at-a-glance.pdf.

2. Deere's estimate of $40 per acre as summarized in its "2020 Sustainability Report" is only for the eight technologies already deployed. (For more, see https://www.deere.com/assets/pdfs/common/our-company/sustainability/sustainability-report-2020.pdf.) The expectations are that the fusion future would allow Deere to potentially target more than $150 billion in addressable markets across industries.

3. "2023 Deere & Company at a Glance."

4. "John Deere Technology and Innovation," John Deere, accessed October 17, 2023, https://www.deere.com/international/en/our-company/innovation/.

5. This point is discussed in detail in Vijay Govindarajan's book *The Three-Box Solution* (Boston: Harvard Business Review Press, 2016.)

6. This idea, sometimes referred to as Amara's Law, is attributed to Roy Amara, a past president of the Institute for the Future.

7. For more discussion, see Venkat Venkatraman's book *The Digital Matrix: New Rules for Business Transformation through Technology* (Los Angeles: LifeTree Media, 2017). Specifically, the argument is that companies should continually focus on identifying activities that could be done by powerful computing machines so that smart human resources can be directed to areas where humans and

machines in collaboration are more likely to be effective than humans or machines independently.

8. In 2022 John Deere announced a request for proposals for satellite communications opportunities. See https://www.deere.com/en/news/all-news/john-deere-announces-request-for-proposals-for-satellite-communications-opportunity.

Appendix

1. Michael S. Scott Morton, ed., *The Corporation of the 1990s: Information Technology and Organizational Transformation* (New York: Oxford University Press, 1991). See also N. Venkatraman, "IT-Enabled Business Transformation: From Automation to Business Scope Redefinition," *MIT Sloan Management Review* 35, no. 2 (Winter 1994).

2. Michael E. Porter and Victor E. Millar, "How Information Gives You Competitive Advantage," *Harvard Business* Review, July 1985.

3. Tim Berners-Lee, "Information Management: A Proposal," March 1989, Word document, https://www.w3.org/History/1989/proposal.html.

4. John C. Henderson and H. Venkatraman, "Strategic Alignment: Leveraging Information Technology for Transforming Organizations," *IBM Systems Journal* 32, no. 1 (1993): 4–16. See also Irving Wladawsky-Berger, "Turning Points in Information Technology," *IBM Systems Journal* 38, nos. 2 and 3 (1999): 449–452.

5. N. Venkatraman, "Five Steps to a Dot-Com Strategy: How to Find Your Footing on the Web," *MIT Sloan Management Review* 41, no. 3 (Spring 2000): 15-28; Vijay Govindarajan and Chris Trimble, *Ten Rules for Strategic Innovators: From Idea to Execution* (Boston: Harvard Business School Press, 2005); Vijay Govindarajan, *The Three-Box Solution: A Strategy for Leading Innovation* (Boston: Harvard Business Review Press, 2016).

6. For an overview of platforms, see Geoffrey G. Parker, Marshall W. Van Alstyne, and Sangeet Paul Choudary, *Platform Revolution: How Networked Markets Are Transforming the Economy—and How to Make Them Work for You* (New York: W. W. Norton & Co., 2016) and Michael A. Cusumano, Annabelle Gawer, and David B. Yoffie, *The Business of Platforms: Strategy in the Age of Digital Competition, Innovation, and Power* (New York: Harper Business, 2019).

7. For recent discussions on ecosystems, see Ron Adner, *Winning the Right Game: How to Disrupt, Defend, and Deliver in a Changing World* (Cambridge: MIT Press, 2021) and Mohan Subramaniam, *The Future of Competitive Strategy: Unleashing the Power of Data and Digital Ecosystems* (Cambridge: MIT Press, 2022).

8. Anandhi Bharadwaj et al., "Digital Business Strategy: Toward a Next Generation of Insights," *MIS Quarterly* 37, no. 2 (June 2013): 471–482.

9. Venkat Venkatraman, *The Digital Matrix: New Rules for Business Transformation through Technology* (Los Angeles: LifeTree Media, 2017); David L. Rogers, *The Digital Transformation Playbook: Rethink Your Business for the Digital Age* (New York: Columbia Business School Publishing, 2016); Sunil Gupta, *Driving Digital Strategy: A Guide to Reimagining Your Business* (Boston: Harvard Business Review Press, 2018); Marco Iansiti and Karim R. Lakhani, *Competing in the Age of*

AI: Strategy and Leadership When Algorithms and Networks Run the World (Boston: Harvard Business Review Press, 2020); Robert Siegel, *The Brains and Brawn Company: How Leading Organizations Blend the Best of Digital and Physical* (New York: McGraw-Hill, 2021); Stephanie L. Woerner, Peter Weill, and Ina M. Sebastian, *Future Ready: The Four Pathways to Capturing Digital Value* (Boston: Harvard Business Review Press, 2022); Thomas H. Davenport and Nitin Mittal, *All-in on AI: How Smart Companies Win Big with Artificial Intelligence* (Boston: Harvard Business Review Press, 2023).

10. Vijay Govindarajan and Jeffrey R. Immelt, "The Only Way Manufacturers Can Survive," *MIT Sloan Management Review* (Spring 2019).

11. Michael Chui et al., "The Economic Potential of Generative AI: The Next Productivity Frontier," McKinsey & Co., June 14, 2023.

INDEX

ACKNOWLEDGMENTS

We are both business strategists with complementary expertise in innovation and transformation, and we have followed each other's professional careers since the mid-1980s. We came together to collaborate on this book project five years back. VG had published *The Three Box Solution* and became convinced that the third box was all about digital. Venkat, who had been researching and teaching at the intersection of strategy and digital (since the late 1980s, when it was called IT), had published *The Digital Matrix* with the conviction that every company will, sooner rather than later, become digital and compete against born-digital firms.

When we got together, we quickly agreed that there is still much apprehension about the role of digital in industrial companies. We reasoned that while many books have been written on digital, and although digital transformation is an overused phrase, there was still an urgent need for a book that focused on industrial companies. To Venkat, trained as a mechanical engineer, this sounded logical; he didn't need any more convincing.

Our collaboration has been strengthened by several shared beliefs and values. We believe that the best business school research has both rigor and relevance. We are inspired by ideas but strive for ideas with impact. We want both to advance theory and to advance solutions to problems that real managers face in real companies. Finally, we are both passionate about the central research question addressed in this book: How can asset-heavy industrial companies leverage real-time data and AI to create new pockets of value?

We could not have completed this book without numerous contributions from a great many people.

Dozens of busy CEOs, COOs, CDOs, and CIOs from the following companies shared their thoughts and observations with us: Ford, Dover, Danaher, Mercedes-Benz, John Deere, DJI, GE, GM, Honeywell, Mahindra & Mahindra, Rolls-Royce, Samsung, Siemens, LIXIL, TVS Motor, and Whirlpool.

A project of this scale and scope requires resources. VG would like to thank Matt Slaughter, dean of the Tuck School of Business, for his generous financial support. Venkat would like to thank Susan Fournier, dean of the Questrom School of Business, and the financial support provided by the David J. McGrath Jr. professorship to complete the book.

We were lucky to have an outstanding editorial team for the book. Anand Raman helped recast our research in an engaging style and has been instrumental in focusing on the key issues during executive interviews and in the framing of arguments. And at HBR Press, we were fortunate to work with Kevin Evers, who sharpened our arguments and made the book go from good to great.

From VG: I would like to thank my family. Kirthi, my wife and best friend, has been both my most perceptive critic and my strongest defender. My daughters, Tarunya and Pasy, and my sons-in-law, Adam Stepinski and Michael Mirandi, are digitally savvy, and conversations with them shaped my thinking about fusion strategies. I sincerely appreciate their kindness, compassion, and love. Without their unfailing encouragement and support, the countless hours invested in this effort could not have come to fruition.

From Venkat: A book project takes a toll on family life. My sincere and loving thanks to my wife, Meera, for her steadfast encouragement to complete this book, as she knew how much this topic meant to me as an engineer who has morphed into a digital strategy academic.

Finally, we would like to thank you for reading our book. We hope you can use *Fusion Strategy* insights as sparks to accelerate your organization's journey to win in your fusion future.

ABOUT THE AUTHORS

VIJAY GOVINDARAJAN (VG) is widely regarded as one of the world's leading experts on strategy and innovation. He is the Coxe Distinguished Professor (a Dartmouth-wide faculty chair) at the Tuck School of Business at Dartmouth College; a faculty partner at Mach49, a Silicon Valley incubator; a former Marvin Bower Fellow at Harvard Business School; and a former faculty member at INSEAD (Fontainebleau) and the Indian Institute of Management (Ahmedabad).

VG has been identified as a leading management thinker in influential publications including: Outstanding Faculty, named by *BusinessWeek* in its Guide to Best B-Schools; a Top Ten Business School Professor in Corporate Executive Education, named by *BusinessWeek*; a Top Five Most Respected Executive Coach on Strategy, rated by *Forbes*; a Rising Superstar, cited by the *Economist*; and an Outstanding Teacher of the Year, voted by MBA students. In 2011 VG was named by Thinkers50 as the number three management thinker in the world and received the Breakthrough Idea Award. In 2019 he was inducted into the Thinkers50 Hall of Fame and was given the Innovation Award for most contributions to the understanding of innovation. VG is one of a select few who have received Thinkers50 Distinguished Achievement Awards in two categories.

He is the rare academic who has published more than twenty-five articles in top academic journals (*Academy of Management Journal, Academy of Management Review, Strategic Management Journal*) and more than twenty-five articles in prestigious practitioner journals.

While serving as the first professor in residence and chief innovation consultant at GE, he worked with then-CEO Jeff Immelt to write "How GE Is Disrupting Itself," the *Harvard Business Review* (HBR) article that introduced the concept of reverse innovation. In its November 2012 issue, HBR picked reverse innovation as one of the great moments in management in the past century. VG's HBR articles "Engineering Reverse Innovations" and "Stop the Innovation Wars" both won the McKinsey Award for the best article published in HBR each year, and his HBR articles "How GE Is Disrupting Itself" and "The CEO's Role in Business Model Reinvention" are among the magazine's fifty bestselling articles of all time. He is also the coauthor of the *New York Times* and *Wall Street Journal* bestseller *Reverse Innovation*.

The recipient of numerous awards for excellence in research, VG was inducted into the *Academy of Management Journal*'s Hall of Fame and ranked by *Management International Review* as one of the Top Twenty North American Superstars for research in strategy. One of his papers was recognized as one of the ten most-cited articles in the fifty-year history of *Academy of Management Journal*.

He has worked with CEOs and top management teams in more than 40 percent of the *Fortune* 500 to discuss, challenge, and escalate their thinking about strategy. His clients include Boeing, Coca-Cola, Colgate, John Deere, FedEx, GE, HP, IBM, JPMorgan Chase, Johnson & Johnson, the *New York Times*, Procter & Gamble, Sony, and Walmart. He has been a keynote speaker at the Bloomberg CEO Forum, the World Business Forum, TED, and the World Economic Forum's annual meeting in Davos.

VG received his doctorate from Harvard Business School and was awarded the Robert Bowne Prize for the best thesis proposal. He received his MBA with distinction from Harvard Business School and his chartered accountancy degree in India, where he was awarded the President's Gold Medal for obtaining the first rank nationwide.

You can follow VG on LinkedIn and X/Twitter @vgovindarajan.

VENKAT VENKATRAMAN is widely regarded as a leading global authority on digital strategy. He is the David J. McGrath Jr. Professor in Management at Boston University's Questrom School of Business, where he holds a joint appointment in the Department of Information Systems and the Department of Strategy and Innovation.

He previously taught strategy at the MIT Sloan School of Management and London Business School. Venkat has an undergraduate degree in mechanical engineering from the Indian Institute of Technology Kharagpur; an MBA from the Indian Institute of Management in Calcutta, where he is a distinguished alumnus; and a PhD in strategic management from the University of Pittsburgh.

His doctoral thesis was awarded the Academy of Management's A. T. Kearney Prize, and the paper from the thesis that published in *Management Science* is one of the most-cited strategy papers in the history of the journal. He is one of the most highly cited researchers in management and digital strategy, according to Google Scholar, with over fifty thousand citations. Stanford University recently placed him among the top 2 percent of scientists based on his citation record. His work on business-IT alignment that was published in *IBM Systems Journal* was judged to be a turning point in IBM's understanding of IT strategy, and his 1986 article in *Management Science* is one of the top fifty articles in the history of the journal. In 2023, he received the INFORMS Information Systems Society Distinguished Fellow Award for "individuals who have made outstanding intellectual contributions to the information systems discipline."

Venkat writes papers for both academic publications and managerial audiences. His academic research has been published in *Management Science, Strategic Management Journal, Information Systems Research, Academy of Management Journal, Academy of Management Review,* and others. His articles for managers have been published in *Harvard Business Review, MIT Sloan Management Review, California Management Review, Business Strategy Review,* and the *Financial Times.*

Over the last three decades, Venkat's research and teaching have focused on how companies win in the digital age, where products, processes, and services are shaped and supported by digital technologies. His 2017 book, *The Digital Matrix: New Rules for Business Transformation through Technology,* has been endorsed by the CEOs of IBM, Verizon, and WPP as well as several CIOs and CDOs.

Venkat has consulted with and delivered presentations and workshops globally to companies such as IBM, Ericsson, GE, BP, Merck, GM, Amazon Web Services, FedEx, Microsoft, McKinsey & Company, WPP, Sony, Tesco, and others. He served as a member of the Digital Technology Advisory Group at Canal+ in Paris for six years.

Contact Venkat on LinkedIn and X/Twitter @NVenkatraman.